Maths

Assessment Practice

Book 1

Ages 10–11+ Years 5–6

J M Bond & Andy Baines

Great Clarendon Street, Oxford, OX2 6DP, United Kingdom

Oxford University Press is a department of the University of Oxford. It furthers the University's objective of excellence in research, scholarship, and education by publishing worldwide. Oxford is a registered trade mark of Oxford University Press in the UK and in certain other countries

First published in 2020
This edition published 2024

British Library Cataloguing in Publication Data
Data available

978-1-38-205408-9

10 9 8 7 6 5 4 3 2 1

Printed in the UK

The manufacturing process conforms to the environmental regulations of the country of origin

Acknowledgements

Content Development Adviser and Reviewer: Jane Cooney
Page make-up: QBS
Cover illustrations: Lo Cole
Illustrations: QBS and Tech-Set Limited

Although we have made every effort to trace and contact all copyright holders before publication this has not been possible in all cases. If notified, the publisher will rectify any errors or omissions at the earliest opportunity.

Contents

Welcome

The 11+ exam is used by grammar schools and selective independent schools for entrance into Year 7. It assesses a child in verbal, non-verbal, English and mathematical reasoning, although individual schools may not test all four subjects, and they may combine some of the subjects together. The 11+ covers English and maths topics that a child will be familiar with from the National Curriculum, but supplements these with verbal reasoning and non-verbal reasoning questions.

Bond offers a complete, flexible programme of preparation materials that you can adapt to your child's specific needs and to the requirements of the exam, or exams.

Do remember to keep checking in with your school of choice so that you know which exam they are using. Schools change their exam boards from time to time. When sitting the actual test, there may be an additional time allowance for candidates needing additional support or an exam in a different format, so do also check with your prospective school if your child needs this. Every child has the right to access the 11+ exam and schools will do all that they can to support you.

Is This Book For a Specific Exam Board?

Unless signalled on the front cover as being geared towards a specific exam board, all Bond 11+ Maths materials are designed to hone the flexibility of approach essential to overcoming the challenges of any 11+ exam. They are also useful preparation for Key Stage 2 SATS exams. The Bond system provides learning, information, and consolidation so that children have an extended, rich education. Our aim is to familiarise children with the type of questions they will find in the exam and to give them the transferable skills that will allow a child to attempt any question in any exam.

As different exam boards and schools may have different question types, the 11+ can be challenging to prepare for. This book can be used as preparation for all exam boards as it provides a wide selection of question types and an enriched education is the best preparation. We help children to both master the techniques and develop the logic and rationale to tackle any unknown question types.

If your child has been working towards an exam from a specific exam board and then the board used by your chosen school changes, all is not lost. This book is good preparation for whichever exam board is being used and the skills covered can be applied to any 11+ exam or independent school entrance exam. It is equally useful for pupils just looking for an extra challenge or wishing to prepare for secondary school.

A Note on Question Formats

The majority of 11+ exams now use multiple-choice answer format (where your child chooses their answer from a list of options), either entirely or for most of their questions. In Bond practice materials, your child will encounter both multiple-choice questions and some in 'standard format', which is where they have to write or type the answer into a box. We continue to use both because, whilst on the one hand it is good to practice the format faced in the exam, standard format questions are proven to be more effective for learning and practice. When a child has to decide on an answer themselves without being given options, the simple act of writing out their answer makes their brain work a bit harder and helps those important skills to get stuck in their memory, ready to be used when they sit down for the real test itself.

How Else Can I Prepare for the 11^{+} Exam?

Bond has a wide range of books and resources to support learning. These include the *10 Minute Test* books and the *Puzzle* series. Bond Online provides a fun way for your child to consolidate their learning and we offer subscriptions which harness adaptive technology, perfect for building confidence.

KEY STUDY SKILLS

Working towards an entrance exam can be an exciting challenge. It is the chance to learn new things and to prepare for secondary school. Here are some tips to help your child:

- Create a study schedule so that your child has a regular routine.
- Balance short bursts of practice with longer assessment papers.
- Create a quiet study space with pencils, an eraser, paper for working out, books and a notebook for writing down techniques. If they study in different places, keep everything in a box that they can take with you.
- Encourage your child to write down strategies to solve new topics.
- Limit distractions such as television, technology and games when they are studying.
- Remind your child that errors are useful. They are part of the journey to success.

A Note for Parents

Parents have a crucial role in helping children and motivating them. Here are some ways that you can really make a difference.

- Check your child is working at the right level. The goal is being able to score 85% on average. It's demotivating if they can't complete questions. It is also important that they work through the system so they are at the right level for the exam at the right time.
- Mark work promptly and go through errors. If papers have not been marked, a child has no idea how they are doing or whether they are repeating the same mistakes.
- Use the *Bond Handbooks* to help your child understand new techniques.
- Limit the range of homework you give your child. The best results are achieved by a system that gradually increases in difficulty. Completing lots of books and papers doesn't guarantee your child's success and often creates stress.
- If your child is struggling with something specific, add additional support in that area. Use *Bond 10 Minute Tests* for consolidation.
- Communication is key. Encourage your child to focus on the positive. No exam is going to ask for 100%, so pushing for that is unrealistic and stressful.
- If your child is constantly struggling, be realistic about whether a selective education is the right choice at this point in time. Many children move to a selective school for their GCSEs or A levels so not going to a selective school now doesn't mean they never will. It is about finding the best school for your child.

How to Use This Book

This book includes many step-by-step techniques for solving different question types. If further support is needed it can be used alongside one or more of the *Bond Handbooks*, which offer insights into the full range of questions that might occur in the exam.

- The first section of the book is made up of Learning Papers that focus on key skills with worked examples then lots of questions for consolidation.
- The second section of the book is made up of Mixed Papers so that children continue to consolidate and do not forget what they have learnt.
- The final section includes two full Test Papers, which can be broken down into shorter sections for more focussed practice, or can be used as full mock tests for that all important exam practice.
- There is an 11+ study guide at the back of the book with some useful hints and tips.
- The removable booklet attached to the back cover includes fully worked out answers to explain how an answer has been reached.

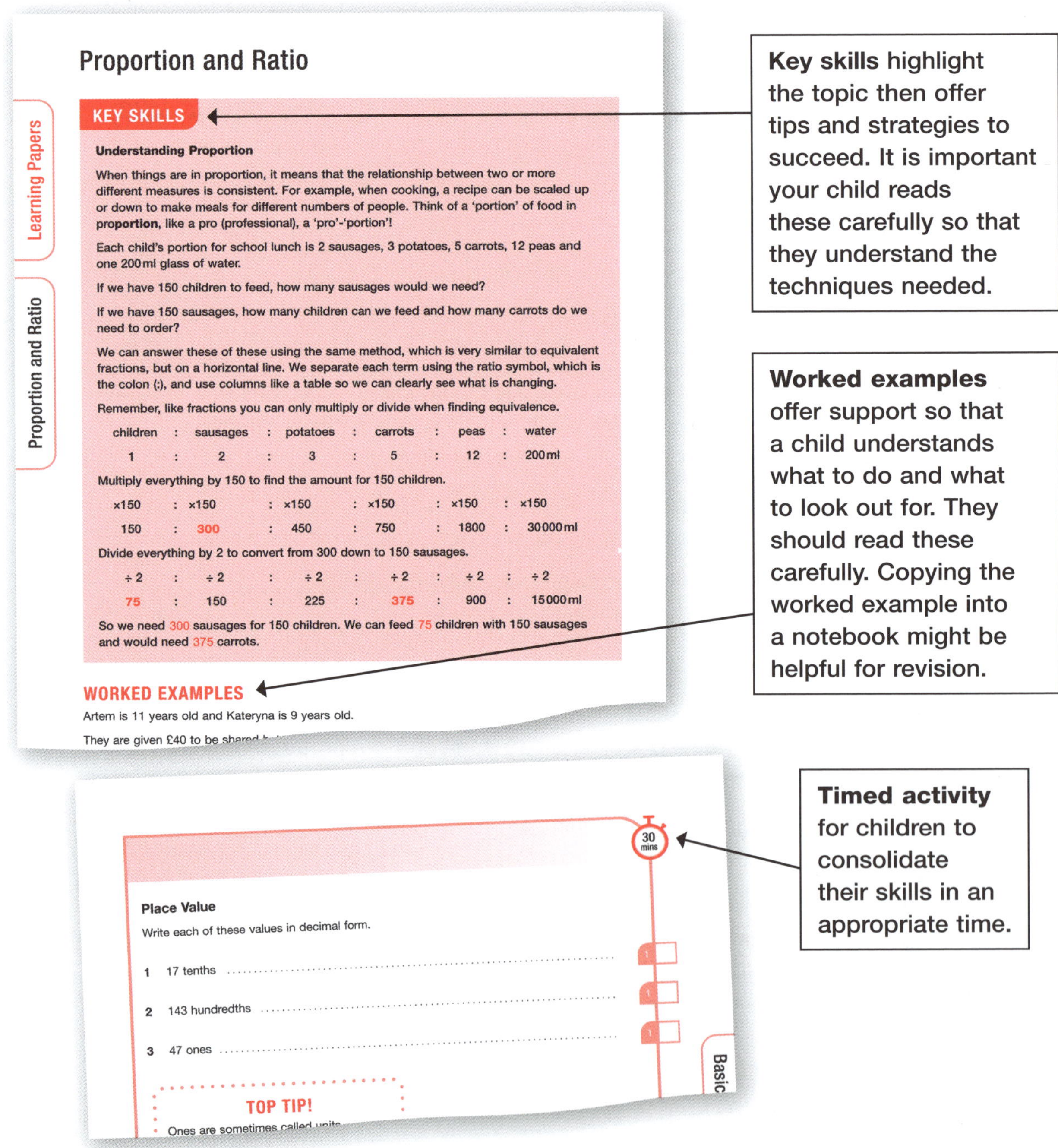

Learning Papers

Proportion and Ratio

Proportion and Ratio

KEY SKILLS

Understanding Proportion

When things are in proportion, it means that the relationship between two or more different measures is consistent. For example, when cooking, a recipe can be scaled up or down to make meals for different numbers of people. Think of a 'portion' of food in **proportion**, like a pro (professional), a 'pro'-'portion'!

Each child's portion for school lunch is 2 sausages, 3 potatoes, 5 carrots, 12 peas and one 200 ml glass of water.

If we have 150 children to feed, how many sausages would we need?

If we have 150 sausages, how many children can we feed and how many carrots do we need to order?

We can answer these of these using the same method, which is very similar to equivalent fractions, but on a horizontal line. We separate each term using the ratio symbol, which is the colon (:), and use columns like a table so we can clearly see what is changing.

Remember, like fractions you can only multiply or divide when finding equivalence.

children	:	sausages	:	potatoes	:	carrots	:	peas	:	water
1	:	2	:	3	:	5	:	12	:	200 ml

Multiply everything by 150 to find the amount for 150 children.

×150	:	×150	:	×150	:	×150	:	×150	:	×150
150	:	300	:	450	:	750	:	1800	:	30 000 ml

Divide everything by 2 to convert from 300 down to 150 sausages.

÷ 2	:	÷ 2	:	÷ 2	:	÷ 2	:	÷ 2	:	÷ 2
75	:	150	:	225	:	375	:	900	:	15 000 ml

So we need 300 sausages for 150 children. We can feed 75 children with 150 sausages and would need 375 carrots.

WORKED EXAMPLES

Artem is 11 years old and Kateryna is 9 years old.

They are given £40 to be shared ...

Place Value

Write each of these values in decimal form.

1 17 tenths ....

2 143 hundredths ....

3 47 ones ....

TOP TIP!

Ones are sometimes called units ...

Basic

KEY MATHS SKILLS

This Bond 11+ Maths Assessment Practice book is useful for all 11+ exams. The Learning Papers cover the following key skills:

- **Numbers** – adding, subtracting, multiplying and dividing, number lines, writing numbers, place value, order and compare, prime/square/cube numbers and roots, fractions, decimals and percentages, patterns and sequences, word problems.
- **Measurements** – unit conversions, mass, area, length, volume, money, time.
- **Statistics** – line charts, bar charts, pie charts, Venn diagrams, pictograms, averages.
- **Problem solving** – bus or train timetables, logic questions, multi-step problems, ratio and proportion, scale problems.
- **Geometry** – 2D and 3D shapes, area and perimeter of shapes, angles, coordinates, symmetry, translations.
- **Algebra** – BIDMAS, simple algebraic equations, simple substitution.

The Mixed Papers ensure the key skills are consolidated thoroughly, then the Test Papers give children the opportunity to get used to the exam process as a natural progression of each book. Don't forget that a rounded education is key. Your child should get used to reading graphs, timetables, and charts. They can try doing sudoku and number games, play online games like Tetris, Snake or Road Blocks and do some logic and number puzzles – Bond has a number puzzle book to make this more fun. There are plenty of times tables apps to ensure your child's basic skills are fast and accurate and games such as Pet Bingo, Marble Maths, and Squeebles Maths Race are great for consolidating skills. Hacker Can is excellent if you want to develop maths and logic skills through learning to programme.

Each book is part of the Bond system with books increasing gradually in difficulty. Once your child has completed this book, there is a clear progression in starting the next book age band if your child has an average score of 85% in this book. If they have achieved an average score of 70% – 85%, then another book at this same age band will provide further support. If your child has achieved an average score of less than 70%, then moving down an age band will be most useful. Once your child has then developed the skills needed at this lower age band, they can then move up with confidence. It is often better to begin at a lower age band to build confidence as your child learns and develops their 11+ skills.

Basic Number Skills

KEY SKILL

Place value

You need to know the **value** of a digit wherever it appears in a number.

1234.5 and 0.123 are shown in this place value grid.

thousands	hundreds	tens	ones	decimal point	tenths	hundredths	thousandths
1	2	3	4	·	5		
			0	·	1	2	3

1234.5 has **3** tens and **5** tenths.

Remember 10 tenths = 1, 100 hundredths = 1, 1000 thousandths = 1.

Special numbers

Factors of a number are numbers that divide into it with no remainder. For example, 1, 2, 4 and 8 are all factors of 8.

Multiples are just extended times tables. A multiple of a number is the answer when the number is multiplied by another number.

Prime numbers are whole numbers greater than 1 that have only 2 factors: 1 and the number itself. **Prime factors** are factors of a number that are also prime numbers, for example, 2 and 3 are prime factors of 12.

Composite numbers are numbers that have more than 2 factors, so they can be divided by 1, the number itself and at least 1 other number.

Square numbers are made by multiplying a number by itself.

Cube numbers are made by multiplying a number by itself 3 times.

Powers are the number of times a number is multiplied by itself, for example 3 to the power of 4 is $3^4 = 3 \times 3 \times 3 \times 3$.

Negative numbers are less than zero and are shown with a minus symbol in front of the number.

	multiples	factors	prime factors	composite	prime	squared number	cubed number
1	1, 2, 3, …	1				1 × 1	1 × 1 × 1
2	2, 4, 6, …	1, 2	2		1 × 2		
3	3, 6, 9, …	1, 3	3		1 × 3		
4	4, 8, 12, …	1, 2, 4	2 × 2	1, 2, 4		2 × 2	
5	5, 10, 15, …	1, 5	5		1 × 5		
6	6, 12, 18, …	1, 2, 3, 6	2 × 3	1, 2, 3, 6			
7	7, 14, 21, …	1, 7	7		1 × 7		
8	8, 16, 24, …	1, 2, 4, 8	2 × 2 × 2	1, 2, 4, 8			2 × 2 × 2
9	9, 18, 27, …	1, 3, 9	3 × 3	1, 3, 9		3 × 3	
10	10, 20, 30, …	1, 2, 5, 10	2 × 5	1, 2, 5, 10			
11							
12							

Can you complete the table for 11 and 12 or two other numbers of your choice?

WORKED EXAMPLES

When calculating with the four operations, we can use column methods, but we can also look to break calculations down to do them mentally.

Addition

$$\begin{array}{r} 887 \\ 998 \\ +\ 776 \\ \hline \mathbf{2661} \\ \hline {\scriptstyle 2\ 2\ 2} \end{array}$$

To add 887, 998 and 776 mentally, break each number into hundreds, tens and ones.

887 = 800 + 80 + 7

998 = 900 + 90 + 8

776 = 700 + 70 + 6

Add the hundreds. 800 + 900 + 700 = 2400. Add the tens. 80 + 90 + 70 = 240.
Add the ones. 7 + 8 + 6 = 21. Now add them altogether. 2 400 + 240 + 21 = **2661**

Basic Number Skills

Learning Papers

Multiplication

```
   3 7 8
×      9
 3 4 0 2
   7 7
```

You can break 378 down into hundreds, tens and ones, and then use factors to mentally calculate the multiplication.

$300 \times 9 = 3 \times 9 \times 100 = 27 \times 100 = 2700$

$70 \times 9 = 7 \times 9 \times 10 = 63 \times 10 = 630$

$8 \times 9 = 8 \times 9 \times 1 = 72$

$378 \times 9 = 2\,700 + 630 + 72 = 2\,000 + 700 + 600 + 30 + 70 + 2 =$ **3402**

Division

```
     0  2  3  4
12 ) 2 ²8 ⁴0 ⁴8
     2  4
        4  0
        3  6
           4  8
           4  8
              0
```

You can also break down the division calculation using factors. 2808 can be rewritten as 2 × 1404 and 12 as 2 × 6. You can then take this further with prime factors, so 2 × 1404 becomes 2 × 2 × 702 and 2 × 6 becomes 2 × 2 × 3. Cancelling out the two sets of 2 × 2 leaves you with 702 ÷ 3. You can then break 702 down into numbers that are easily divisible by 3.

$\frac{2808}{12} = \frac{2 \times 1404}{2 \times 6} = \frac{2 \times 2 \times 702}{2 \times 2 \times 3} = \frac{702}{3} = \frac{300 + 300 + 90 + 12}{3}$ $100 + 100 + 30 + 4 =$ **234**

Subtraction

103 – 75.2 = **27.8**

```
  9 12   1
1 0 3 · 0
–  7 5 · 2
   2 7 · 8
```

When calculating with decimal numbers, remember to keep the decimal point in line when doing addition or subtraction calculations. You can also adjust the number so that they have an equal number of digits. Here 103.0 is the same as 103.

```
  9 12 1
1 0 3 0   (1, 0 and 3 crossed out)
–  7 5 2
   2 7 8
```

With addition and subtraction of decimals, you can also ignore the decimal point then add it back in.

30 mins

Place Value

Write each of these values in decimal form.

1 17 tenths 1

2 143 hundredths 1

3 47 ones 1

> **TOP TIP!**
> Ones are sometimes called units.

Rounding

Write each of these numbers to the nearest whole number.

4 8.35 1

5 0.71 1

6 4.48 1

7 0.123 1

Using the Four Operations

8 Add together 3.7, 2.95 and 0.187 1

9 Take 1.689 from 3.2 1

10 Divide 799 by 17 1

Learning Papers

Basic Number Skills

Special Numbers

TOP TIP!

A number line can be useful when working out the difference between positive and negative numbers. Positive numbers are to the right of 0 (zero) and are greater than 0, negative numbers are to the left of 0 and less than 0.

On one day in February, the temperatures in different places were as follows.

Chicago	–3°C	Montreal	–10°C	Singapore	31°C
Cape Town	27°C	Miami	26°C	Toronto	–5°C

11 Which was the coldest? 1

12 How much colder was it in Chicago than Cape Town? 1

13 The difference between Toronto and Miami was 1

14 The difference between Singapore and Montreal was 1

TOP TIP!

Multiples are found by repeatedly adding the same number, for example, 7, 14, 21, 28, …

Find the next three multiples of the following numbers.

15 9 ...., ..., ... 1

16 12 ...., ..., ... 1

TOP TIP!

A number is a multiple of 3 if the sum of its digits is a multiple of 3.

For example:

758	7 + 5 + 8 = 20	2 + 0 = 2	758 is NOT a multiple of 3.
558	5 + 5 + 8 = 18	1 + 8 = 9	758 IS a multiple of 3.

17 Which of the following is not a multiple of 3? 27, 36, 43, 57, 66 1

18 What are the **factors** of 21?

.................., ..., ..., ... 4

19 What are the **prime factors** of 60? ...., ..., ... 3

20 What is the next number that is NOT a composite number after 19? 1

21 What is the next number that is NOT a composite number before 61? 1

22 What is the next composite number after 46? 1

$5 \times 5 = 5^2$ $2 \times 2 \times 2 = 2^3$. Now write the following in the same way.

23 $10 \times 10 \times 10 \times 10 =$ 1

24 $7 \times 7 \times 7 =$ 1

25 $1 \times 1 \times 1 \times 1 \times 1 \times 1 =$ 1

Total 30

Basic Number Skills

Decimals, Fractions and Percentages

KEY SKILL

Equivalent Fractions, Decimals and Percentages

It is useful to know how to find equivalents of fractions and mixed numbers. They can be used for addition, subtraction, ordering numbers and when simplifying an answer.

Let us look at some examples. To find a fraction **equivalent** to another fraction, multiply the **numerator** and the **denominator** by the same number.

$$\frac{3}{5} = \frac{3 \times 10}{5 \times 10} = \frac{30}{50} = \frac{30 \times 2}{50 \times 2} = \frac{60}{100}$$

Sometimes, we also want to find equivalent decimals and percentages. To change a fraction into a percentage, find an equivalent fraction with a denominator of 100.

$$\frac{30}{50} = \frac{60}{100} = 60\,\% = 0.60 = 0.6$$

$$\frac{21}{25} = \frac{21 \times 4}{25 \times 4} \times 4 = \frac{84}{100} = 80\% = 0.84$$

You can use multiplication to change a **mixed number** into an **improper fraction** which also helps when finding equivalents.

Change $2\frac{3}{5}$ to an improper fraction by multiplying the denominator (5)
by the whole number (2)
and then adding the numerator of the fraction (3)
to find the numerator of the improper fraction (13), giving a fraction $\frac{13}{5}$.

$$2\frac{3}{5} = \frac{13}{5} = \frac{13 \times 10}{5 \times 10} = \frac{130}{50} = \frac{130 \times 2}{50 \times 2} = \frac{260}{100} = 260\% = 2.60 = 2.6$$

When adding or subtracting fractions, all of the fractions need to have the same denominator, then the numerators are simply added or subtracted according to the calculation required.

We can see that the same quantity can be written in different ways.

$\frac{3}{5} = 60\% = 0.6$ $\quad 2\frac{3}{5} = 260\% = 2.6$ $\quad \frac{21}{25} = 84\% = 0.84$

This makes it easier to answer the following questions.

Which is bigger, $\frac{21}{25}$ or 0.84? The answer is they are the same.

What is $2\frac{3}{5} - 84\%$ written as a decimal? The answer is 260% – 84% = 176% = 1.76.

WORKED EXAMPLES

- Multiply each of these numbers by 10, 100 and 1000: 37.8, 0.047.

  Multiplying by multiples of 10 means the digits stay the same but move one place to the left on a place value grid (or the decimal point moves one place to the right on a place value grid). The same is the case if we multiply by 10 again.

37.8 × 10 = **378**	0.0047 × 10 = **0.047**
37.8 × 100 = **3780**	0.0047 × 100 = **0.47**
37.8 × 1000 = **37800**	0.0047 × 1000 = **4.7**

Similarly, to divide by 10, place the numbers in a place value grid using hundreds, tens, ones, tenths, hundredths, thousandths, etc. Divide a number by 10 by moving the digits one place to the right.

37.8 ÷ 10 = **3.78**

4.7 ÷ 10 = **0.47**

- A person's salary was £36 000. They are given a 5% increase. What is their new salary?

  100% of £36 000 is £36 000.

  10% of £36 000 is £3600.

  5% of £36 000 is £1800.

  A 5% increase is 100% + 5% = £36 000 + £1800 = **£37 800**

- 20% of my money is £2.55. What is $\frac{2}{5}$ of it?

  We need to compare the percentage with the fraction; sometimes it is quicker one way around than the other. With practice, you will choose the best way first time more often.

  $\frac{2}{5} = \frac{2 \times 10}{5 \times 10} = \frac{20}{50} = \frac{40}{100} = 40\%$

  We have 20% and we want 40%, so we can just double the amount.

  20% of my money is £2.55.

  40% of my money is £5.10.

  $\frac{2}{5}$ of my money is **£5.10**.

Decimals, Fractions and Percentages

30 mins

Multiplying and Dividing Decimals by 10, 100 and 1000

Divide each of these numbers by 10.

1 78.65 1

2 6.54 1

3 467.5 1

4 0.123 1

Divide each of the following numbers by 1000.

5 385 1

6 0.12 1

Learning Papers

Decimals, Fractions and Percentages

7 7.8 1

8 49 1

Insert the missing numbers in these calculations.

9 4.9 × .... = 490 1

10 .... ÷ 10 = 0.123 1

11 0.136 × 100 = ... 1

Decimals on a Number Line

Which numbers are the arrows pointing to on this number line?

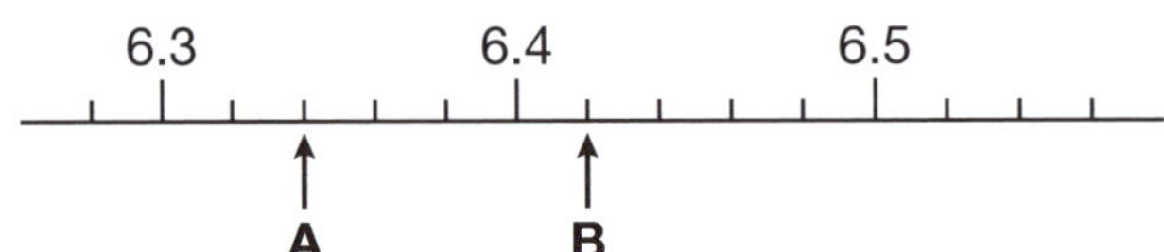

12 Arrow A points to 1

13 Arrow B points to 1

Ordering Decimals

14 Arrange these numbers in order, putting the largest first.

7.8 7.088 7.88 7.008 4

Equivalent Fractions

TOP TIP!

To find equivalent fractions, multiply the **numerator** and the **denominator** by the same number.

$$\frac{2}{3} = \frac{2 \times 2}{3 \times 2} = \frac{2 \times 3}{3 \times 3} = \frac{2 \times 7}{3 \times 7} = \frac{2 \times 40}{3 \times 40}$$

$$\frac{2}{3} = \frac{4}{6} = \frac{6}{9} = \frac{14}{21} = \frac{80}{120}$$

For questions 15–20, fill in the missing numerators to complete the equivalent fractions.

15 $\frac{4}{5} = \frac{\quad}{25}$ 1

16 $\frac{7}{11} = \frac{\quad}{121}$ 1

17 $\frac{7}{8} = \frac{\quad}{64}$ 1

18 $\frac{2}{7} = \frac{\quad}{42}$ 1

19 $\frac{3}{4} = \frac{\quad}{48}$ 1

20 $\frac{7}{9} = \frac{\quad}{63}$ 1

Ordering Fractions

21 Arrange these fractions in order of size, putting the smallest first.

$\frac{1}{2}$ $\frac{2}{3}$ $\frac{5}{6}$ $\frac{3}{8}$ $\frac{3}{4}$

.... 5

Fraction of a Number

22 Last Friday, $\frac{1}{8}$ of the pupils in our school were absent. There are 560 pupils altogether in the school.

There were .... pupils absent and .... pupils present. 2

Adding and Subtracting Fractions

23 $\frac{5}{8} + \frac{7}{16} =$ 1

24 $7 - 4\frac{2}{9} =$ 1

Calculating Percentages

25 There are 30 children in Class 4. 60% of them are girls.

There are .... girls and .... boys. 2

Total 34

Decimals, Fractions and Percentages

Proportion and Ratio

KEY SKILLS

Understanding Proportion

When things are in proportion, it means that the relationship between two or more different measures is consistent. For example, when cooking, a recipe can be scaled up or down to make meals for different numbers of people. Think of a 'portion' of food in pro**portion**, like a pro (professional), a 'pro'-'portion'!

Each child's portion for school lunch is 2 sausages, 3 potatoes, 5 carrots, 12 peas and one 200 ml glass of water.

If we have 150 children to feed, how many sausages would we need?

If we have 150 sausages, how many children can we feed and how many carrots do we need to order?

We can answer these of these using the same method, which is very similar to equivalent fractions, but on a horizontal line. We separate each term using the ratio symbol, which is the colon (:), and use columns like a table so we can clearly see what is changing.

Remember, like fractions you can only multiply or divide when finding equivalence.

children	:	sausages	:	potatoes	:	carrots	:	peas	:	water
1	:	2	:	3	:	5	:	12	:	200 ml

Multiply everything by 150 to find the amount for 150 children.

×150	:	×150	:	×150	:	×150	:	×150	:	×150
150	:	**300**	:	450	:	750	:	1800	:	30 000 ml

Divide everything by 2 to convert from 300 down to 150 sausages.

÷ 2	:	÷ 2	:	÷ 2	:	÷ 2	:	÷ 2	:	÷ 2
75	:	150	:	225	:	**375**	:	900	:	15 000 ml

So we need 300 sausages for 150 children. We can feed 75 children with 150 sausages and would need 375 carrots.

WORKED EXAMPLES

Artem is 11 years old and Kateryna is 9 years old.

They are given £40 to be shared between them in the ratio of their ages.

Artem will get .... Kateryna will get ....

With ratio questions, always add up the values of the ratio parts, then compare this total with the quantity you are dealing with.

So, with this question we are sharing 40 in the ratio 11 to 9.

11 + 9 = 20. 20 goes into 40 two times, so multiply the ratios by 2.

11	:	9	=	20
×2		×2		×2
22	:	18	=	40

Artem will get £22 and Kateryna will get £18.

£1 = 10.75 Norwegian krone	£1 = 8.54 Danish krone
£1 = 1.15 euros	£1 = 1.72 Australian dollars

How many Norwegian krone do you get for £3? .... Norwegian krone

How many euros do you get for £13? .... euros

How many Australian dollars do you get for £50? .... Australian dollars

Using a similar method as above, we can do the following.

£	:	Norwegian krone
1	:	10.75
×3		×3
3	:	10.75 × 3 = 32.25 Norwegian krone

£	:	Euros
1	:	1.15
×13		×13
13	:	1.15 × 13 = 14.95 euros

£	:	Australian dollars
1	:	1.72
×50		×50
50	:	1.72 × 50 = 86 Australian dollars

Learning Papers

Proportion and Ratio

30 mins

Calculating Proportion

1 If 11 items cost £7.37, what would be the cost of 8 items? 1

2 If 9 items cost £6.30, what will be the cost of 11 items? 1

At the supermarket there were various sizes of Marvello.

A	B	C	D	E	F
1 kg	200 g	125 g	250 g	750 g	400 g
£3.81	£1.10	54p	93p	£3.97	£1.56

3 Tin .... was the best bargain. 1

4 Tin .... was the second best. 1

5 Tin .... was the third best. 1

6 If 13 items cost £1.56, what would 7 items cost? 1

1 kg of Britewash costs £1.20. At this price per kg:

7 I could buy .... with £6.00. 1

8 I could buy .... with 30p. 1

9 I would have to pay .... with 3.5 kg. 1

Calculating Ratio

There are 351 children in a school. There are 7 boys to every 6 girls.

10 How many boys are there? 1

11 How many girls are there? 1

12 A cash box contains some coins to the value of £5.25.

There are twice as many 5p coins as 2p coins, and twice as many 2p coins as 1p coins.

This means there are:

.... 5p coins, ... 2p coins and .... 1p coins 3

13 The ages of Grandma, Uncle John and Tom add up to 105 years.

Grandma is twice as old as Uncle John, and Uncle John is twice as old as Tom.

Grandma is .... years old, Uncle John is .... years old and

Tom is .... years old. 3

Dividing Amounts in a Ratio

Thirty-six pencils are shared among A, B and C in the ratio of 1 : 3 : 5. How many pencils does each person have?

14 A has 1

15 B has 1

16 C has 1

17 Emma (who is 8 years old), Salim (who is 7) and Katie (who is 5), share £10.00 in the ratio of their ages.

Emma gets ...., Salim gets .... and Katie gets 3

18 Share 39 sweets among Penny, Ragini and Prue, giving Penny 3 times as much as Ragini, and Ragini 3 times as much as Prue.

Penny has .... sweets, Ragini has .... sweets and Prue has

.... sweets. 3

Total 26

BIDMAS, Sequences and Algebra

KEY SKILLS

Order of Operations

BIDMAS is used to help you remember the order of operations.

1: **B**rackets ( )

2: **I**ndices, or Power or Order $^{2\ 3\ 4}$

3: **D**ivide and **M**ultiply ÷ ×

4: **A**dd and **S**ubtract + –

For now, you will not see indices, so make sure you complete ÷ or × **before** you + or –.

For example: 9 + 6 ÷ 3 = 9 + 2 = 11

Sequences

When you have a sequence, look for patterns in the opposite order to BIDMAS, e.g. look at addition and subtraction before multiplication and division. Ask yourself:

- Are we adding or subtracting the same amount each time?
- Are we multiplying or dividing the same amount each time?
- Are we adding or subtracting the same increasing or decreasing amount each time?
- Are we multiplying or dividing the same increasing or decreasing amount each time?

Solving Equations Using Algebra

Letters are used in algebra to represent missing numbers. Letters instead of a question mark (?) or images, are used to help us, so to make sure we recognise them they are presented in italic and may be in a different font. If $a = 2$ and $b = 3$, what is the value of $a + b$?

If we have more than one of the same unknown, we write the quantity in front (we don't bother with using the number 1).

$9a \quad 4b \quad c \quad p \quad 8q \quad -2r \quad 3x \quad y \quad z$

WORKED EXAMPLES

Work out the following calculations.

$8 \times 2 + 1 =$	$8 \div 2 + 1 =$
$8 + 2 \times 1 =$	$8 + 2 \div 1 =$
$8 \times 2 - 1 =$	$8 \div 2 - 1 =$
$8 - 2 \times 1 =$	$8 - 2 \div 1 =$

The rule is that you must multiply and divide before adding or subtracting. These are shown in bold to help you. This is one of the most important rules in mathematics, so it is important to learn this as soon as possible.

$\mathbf{8 \times 2} + 1 = \mathbf{16} + 1 = 17$	$\mathbf{8 \div 2} + 1 = \mathbf{4} + 1 = 5$
$8 + \mathbf{2 \times 1} = 8 + \mathbf{2} = 10$	$8 + \mathbf{2 \div 1} = 8 + \mathbf{2} = 10$
$\mathbf{8 \times 2} - 1 = \mathbf{16} - 1 = 15$	$\mathbf{8 \div 2} - 1 = \mathbf{4} - 1 = 3$
$8 - \mathbf{2 \times 1} = 8 - \mathbf{2} = 6$	$8 - \mathbf{2 \div 1} = 8 - \mathbf{2} = 6$

When solving or simplifying equations, remember to do exactly the same to BOTH sides of the = sign. You can add, subtract, divide or multiply.

Find the value of x for these equations.

$x + 4 = 7$	$x - 4 = 7$
$4 + x = 7$	$4 - x = 7$

Now, these look very similar, but follow the rule: ***"Whatever you do to one side you must do to the other."***

$$\begin{aligned} x + 4 &= 7 \\ -4 \quad & \quad -4 \\ x &= 3 \end{aligned}$$

Subtract four from both sides.

$$\begin{aligned} x - 4 &= 7 \\ +4 \quad & \quad +4 \\ x &= 11 \end{aligned}$$

Add four to both sides.

$$\begin{aligned} 4 + x &= 7 \\ -4 \quad & \quad -4 \\ x &= 3 \end{aligned}$$

Subtract four from both sides.

$$\begin{aligned} 4 - x &= 7 \\ +x \quad & \quad +x \\ +4 \quad & \quad 7 + x \\ -7 \quad & \quad -7 \\ x &= -3 \end{aligned}$$

You need a positive x so add x to both sides.

Subtract seven from both sides.

Learning Papers

BIDMAS, Sequences and Algebra

30 mins

Sequences

Here is a series of triangles. The first triangle has one row and one dot. The second triangle has 2 rows and 4 (or 2^2) dots. The third triangle has 3 rows and 9 (or 3^2) dots.

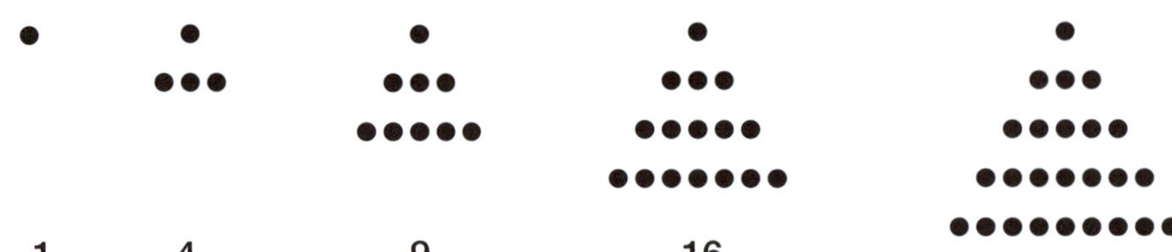

1 How many dots are there in 5 rows? 1

2 If there were 7 rows, how many dots would there be? 1

3 In 11 rows there would be .... dots. 1

4 In 20 rows there would be .... dots. 1

5 A book has 38 lines to each page.
On which page will the 1000th line appear? 1

BIDMAS

Complete these calculations.

6 (7 × 8) + ... = 61 1

7 (9 × 12) − .... = 106 1

8 8 × (7 − ....) = 32 1

9 6 × (11 − ....) = 36 1

Equations with Missing Operations

Put a sign in each space to make these calculations correct.

10 45 .... 7 = 52 1

11 33 .... 3 = 11 1

TOP TIP!

When filling in a missing symbol, you can check your answer by reversing the equation.

12 678 .... 56 = 33968 1

13 90 .... 5 = 18 1

Put a sign in each space to make these calculations correct.

14 74 .... 5 = 14.8 1

15 74 .... 5 = 79 1

16 74 .... 5 = 69 1

17 74 .... 5 = 370 1

Algebra

Which number is represented by each symbol?

18 2 × Δ = 4 × 5 Δ = ... 1

19 5 × ♣ = 27 − 2 ♣ = ... 1

20 ⊗ × 3 = 36 ÷ 3 ⊗ = ... 1

21 ♦ × 4 = 10 + 10 ♦ = ... 1

Find the value of y in the following equations.

22 $3y = 10 - 1$ $y =$ 1

23 $4y - y = 12$ $y =$ 1

24 $2y + y = 6$ $y =$ 1

25 $3y + y = 11 + 1$ $y =$ 1

Total 25

Measures

Learning Papers

Measures

KEY SKILLS

Area, Perimeter and Volume

Perimeter is the distance around the edge of an object. Think about drawing a line around the edge. Calculating the perimeter usually involves adding.

Area is the amount of 2D space an object covers and is counted in square units. Think about shading or colouring an object. Calculating area usually involves multiplying 2 values.

Volume is the amount of 3D space an object takes up and is counted in cube units. Think about filling the object with water. Calculating volume usually involves multiplying 3 values.

Equivalent Measures

It is very useful to be able to use and convert between different units of measure, here are a few of the most used.

1 km = 1 000 m	= 100 000 cm	= 1 000 000 mm
1 km = 1 × 1 000 m	= 1 000 × 100 cm	= 100 000 × 10 mm
1 tonne = 1 000 kg	= 1 000 000 g	
1 tonne = 1 × 1 000 kg	= 1 000 × 1 000 g	
1 litre = 100 cl	= 1 000 ml	
1 litre = 1 × 100 cl	= 100 × 10 ml	
1 m^2 = 10 000 cm^2	= 1 000 000 mm^2	
1 m^2 = 1 × 100 × 100 cm^2	= 10 000 × 10 × 10 mm^2	
1 m^3 = 1 000 000 cm^3	= 1 000 000 000 mm^3	
1 m^3 = 1 × 100 × 100 × 100 cm^3	= 1 000 000 × 10 × 10 × 10 mm^3	

8:45 a.m. = 08:45. Morning times in the 24-hour clock have a.m. missing and 0 at the front if less than 10.

6:45 p.m. = 18:45. Afternoon and evening times in the 24hr clock have p.m. missing and 12 hours adding on.

Midnight in the 24-hour clock is zero hours: 00:00

WORKED EXAMPLES

- Which is more: 10 lb of carrots or 10 kg of carrots?

  1 kg ≈ 2.2 lb

  So 10 kg ≈ 2.2 lb × 10 which is 22 lbs. 22 > 10, so **10 kg is more**.

- Which is shorter: 14 km or 10 miles?

  1 mile ≈ 1.6 km

  10 miles ≈ 1.6 km × 10 ≈ 16 km. 14 < 16 so **14 km is shorter**.

  Which is greater: 2 litres or 2 pints?

  1 litre ≈ 1.75 pints

  So 2 litres ≈ 1.75 pints × 2 ≈ 3.5 pints so **2 litres is more**.

- Mrs Forgetmenot is 9 minutes late for the 9.42 a.m. train. How long will she have to wait for the train at 10.27 a.m.?

  There are 60 minutes in an hour, so from 9.42 a.m. to 10 a.m. there are (60 – 42 = 18) minutes.

  From 10 a.m. to 10.27 a.m. there are 27 minutes.

  She was 9 minutes late, so 18 + 27 – 9 = **36 minutes**.

TOP TIP!

≈ means "is approximately"

Measures

30 mins

Area

Find the area of these triangles.

TOP TIP!

To find the area of a triangle, multiply the height by the length and then divide by 2.

Scale: 1 square = 1 cm^2

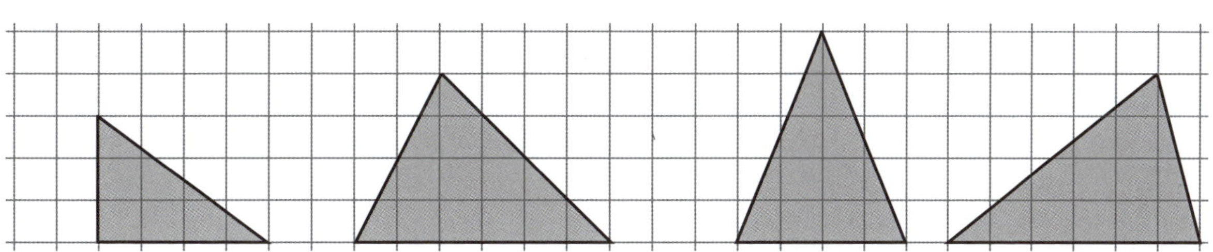

1 .... **2** .... **3** .... **4** ....

4

Looking at the cuboid, what is the area of:

5 side A? 1

6 side B? 1

7 side C? 1

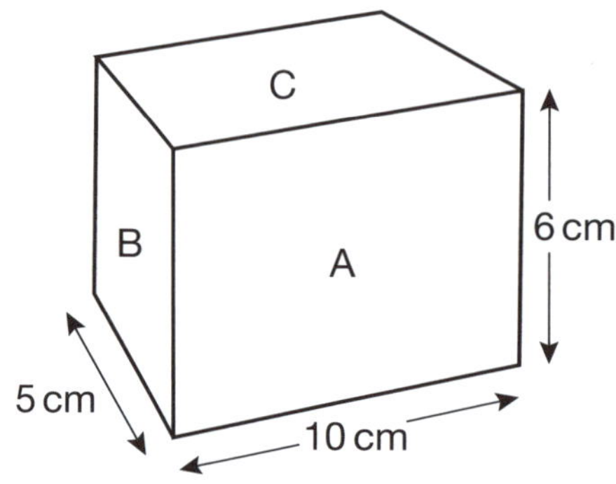

Perimeter

What is the perimeter of:

8 side A? 1

9 side B? 1

10 side C? 1

Volume

11 What is the volume of a 12 cm by 5 cm by 8 cm cuboid in cm^3? .... cm^3 1

12 What is the volume of a 12 cm by 50 mm by 8 cm cuboid in mm^3? .... mm^3 1

13 What is the volume of a 1 m by 80 cm by 1200 mm cuboid in m^3? .... m^3 1

Length

Convert the following lengths to metres.

14 245 cm = ... m

15 1342 cm = ... m 2

16 12 345 cm = ... m 1

Mass

17 What is the difference between 0.225 tonnes and 128 kg? .... kg 1

18 What must be added to 375 g to make 1 kg? .... g 1

Capacity

capacity capacity is the maximum amount that a container can hold.

TOP TIP!

1 litre is 1 000 cm^3

19 How many litres is 450 cm^3? .... litres 1

20 What is the capacity of a container which is a quarter full with 27 litres? .... litres 1

21 A container is a third full with 600 cm^3, what is its capacity? .... litres 1

Time

Using this world time chart, answer the following questions.

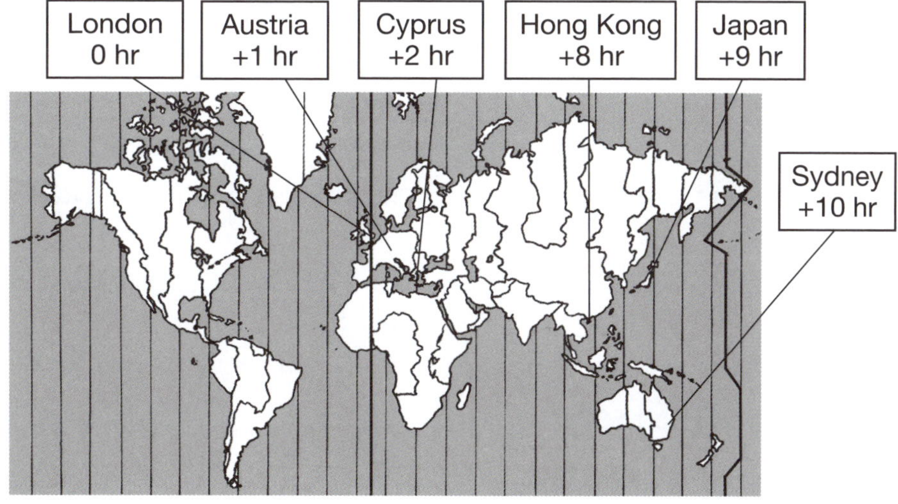

Using a 24-hour clock, when it is midday in Japan it is:

22 .... in London. **23** .... in Hong Kong. 2

24 It is 12:00 midday in Cyprus. Using a 24-hour clock, what time is it in Austria? 1

25 It is 4:36 p.m. in Hong Kong. What time is it in London? 1

Total 25

Measures

Shape, Space, Position and Direction

KEY SKILLS

2D Shapes

Check that you know the properties of these 2D shapes:

- triangles have 3 sides – equilateral, right angled, isosceles, scalene
- quadrilaterals have 4 sides – square, rectangle, parallelogram, rhombus, trapezium, kite
- a hexagon has 6 sides, a heptagon has 7 sides, an octagon has 8 sides and a decagon has 10 sides.

3D Shapes

Check that you know the properties of these 3D shapes and can recognise the nets that can form them: cube, cuboid, cylinder, prism and pyramid.

This is a cube with its net.

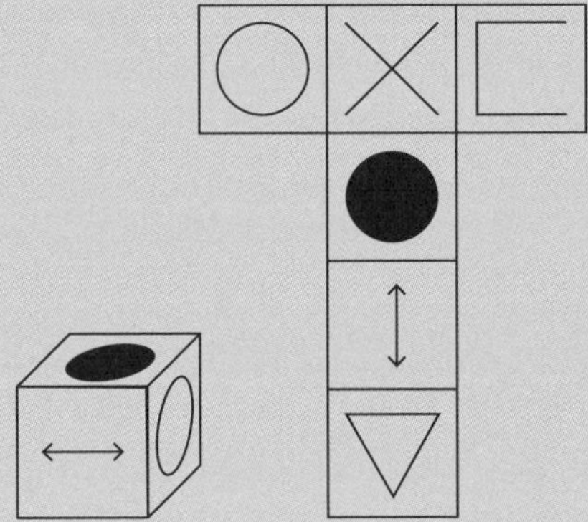

A cube has 6 **faces** (flat sides), 12 **edges** (sections on the edge of a face), and 8 **vertices** (points where edges meet).

Angles

Learn these four basic angle rules:

- angles around a point add up to 360°
- angles on a straight line add up to 180°
- angles in a triangle add up to 180°
- angles in a quadrilateral add up to 360°.

Angles are measured in degrees. A complete rotation is 360 degrees. Direction of rotation can be described as clockwise or anticlockwise.

The hands on a clockface and the points of a compass can be used to describe angles or rotation.

- Between each number on a clockface there is an angle of 30°.
- Between the compass points of N-NE, NE-E, E-SE, and so on there is an angle of 45°.

WORKED EXAMPLE

Plot the points (1, 3), (1, –1), (–3, –1) on the grid below.

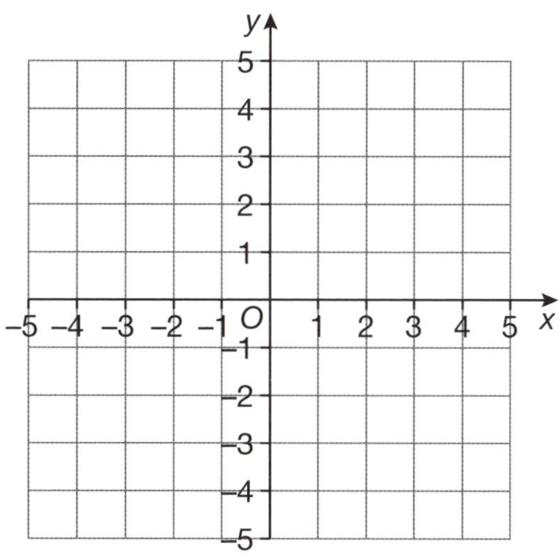

These points are the **vertices** of a square. Mark the fourth **vertex** and draw the square.

The **coordinates** of the fourth vertex are (.............., ...).

The coordinates of the centre of the square are (.............., ...).

Coordinates indicate the position of a point on a graph or grid, for example, (3, 2). The first number is horizontal, the distance you move in the x-direction; the second number is vertical, the distance you move in the y-direction.

A vertex, (plural is vertices) is the point where two or more edges or sides in a shape meet.

The origin is the point (0,0) on a graph.

(1, 3) is 1 to the right and 3 up from the origin.

(1, –1)) is 1 to the right and 1 down from the origin.

(–3, –1)) is 3 to the left and 1 down from the origin.

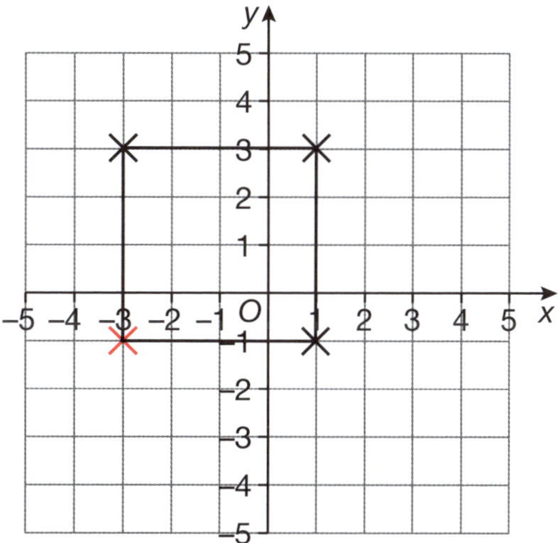

The coordinates of the fourth vertex are **(–3 , 3)**.

The coordinates of the centre of the square are **(–1 , 1)**.

30 mins

Angles

What is the size of the smaller angle:

1 between 1 and 3? 1

2 between 2 and 7? 1

3 between 7 and 11? 1

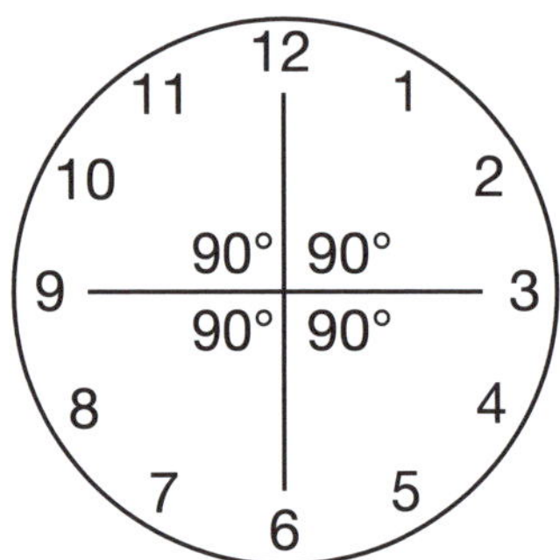

TOP TIP!

Angles on a straight line add up to 180°

4 50°, p° and 45° are all angles on the same straight line, what is the value of p? p° = ... ° 1

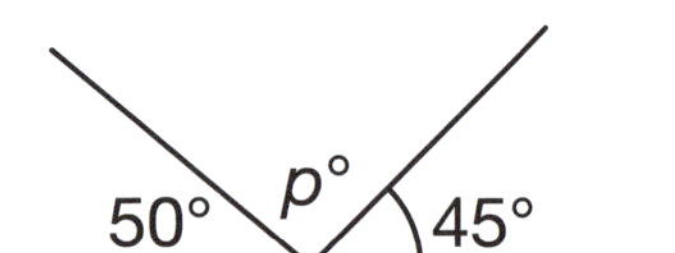

5 All the angles are on the same straight line, what is the value of q? q° = ... ° 1

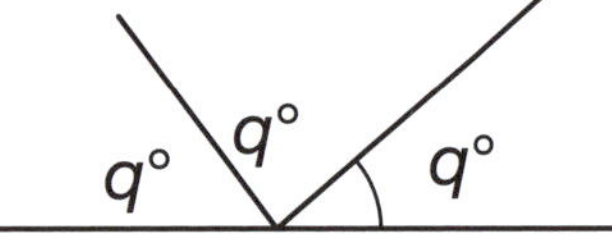

6 All the angles are on the same straight line, what is the value of r? r° = ... ° 1

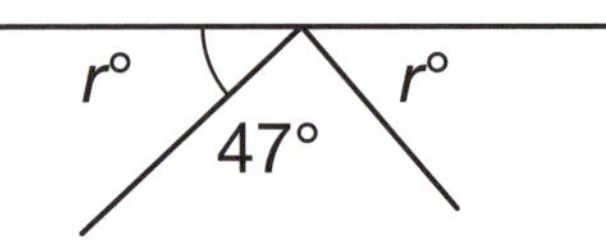

Label the following angles. Choose from: **acute**, **obtuse**, **reflex** or **right angle**.

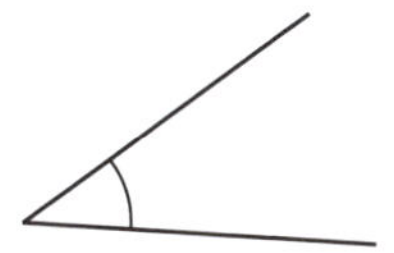

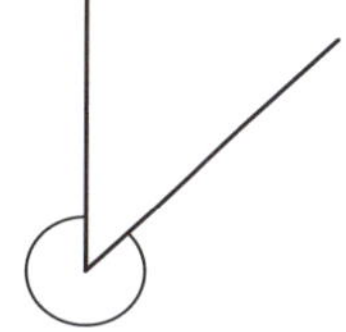

7 .... **8** .... **9** **10** 4

Coordinates

11 Plot the points (3, 5), (–1, 5), (3, –2) on the grid. 3

These points are the vertices of a rectangle. Mark the fourth vertex and draw the rectangle.

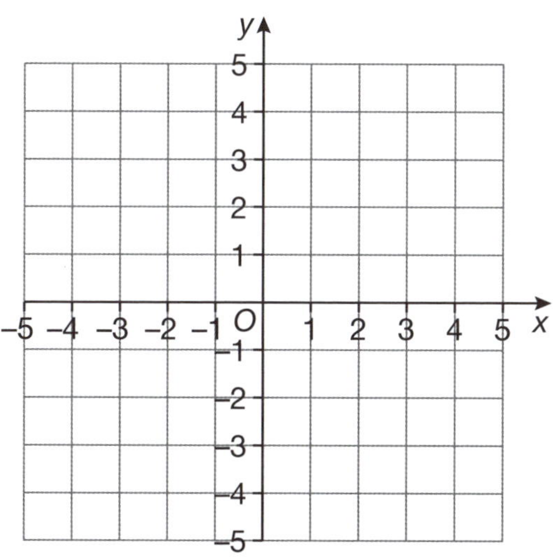

> **TOP TIP!**
>
> When plotting coordinates on a grid, use the rule “along the corridor and up the stairs” to remember to go horizontal, then vertical.

12 The coordinates of the fourth vertex are (.............., ...). 1

2D Shapes

Use these words to help you name the following shapes:

rhombus, **kite**, **parallelogram**, **trapezium**, rectangle.

13 .... **14** .... **15** ....

16 .... **17** 5

3D Shapes

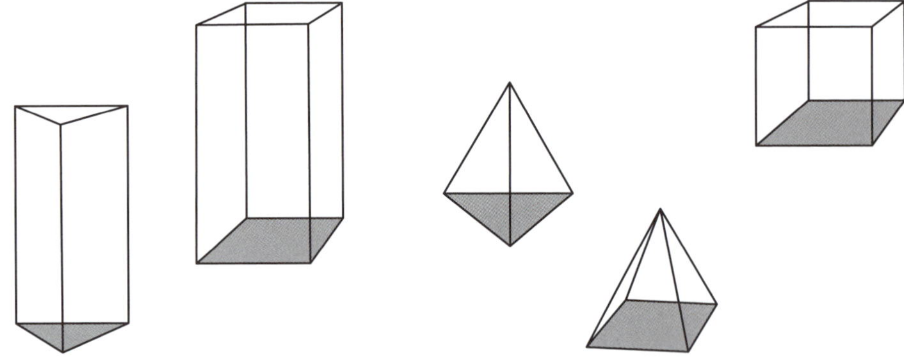

18 Fill in the six missing values.

Name of solid	Number of faces	Number of vertices	Number of edges
Triangular prism			
Square prism			

6

Nets

Here are three shaded cubes.

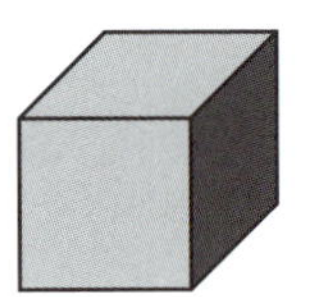

B

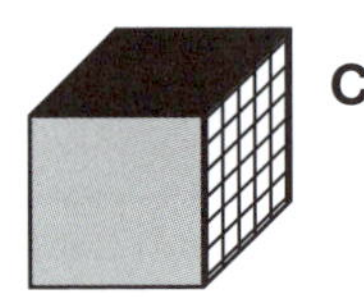

Which cube has the following nets? Choose between A, B, C or none.

19

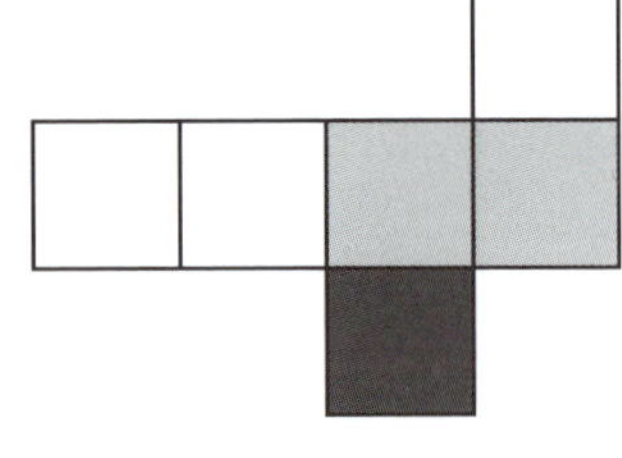

Is 1

20

Is 1

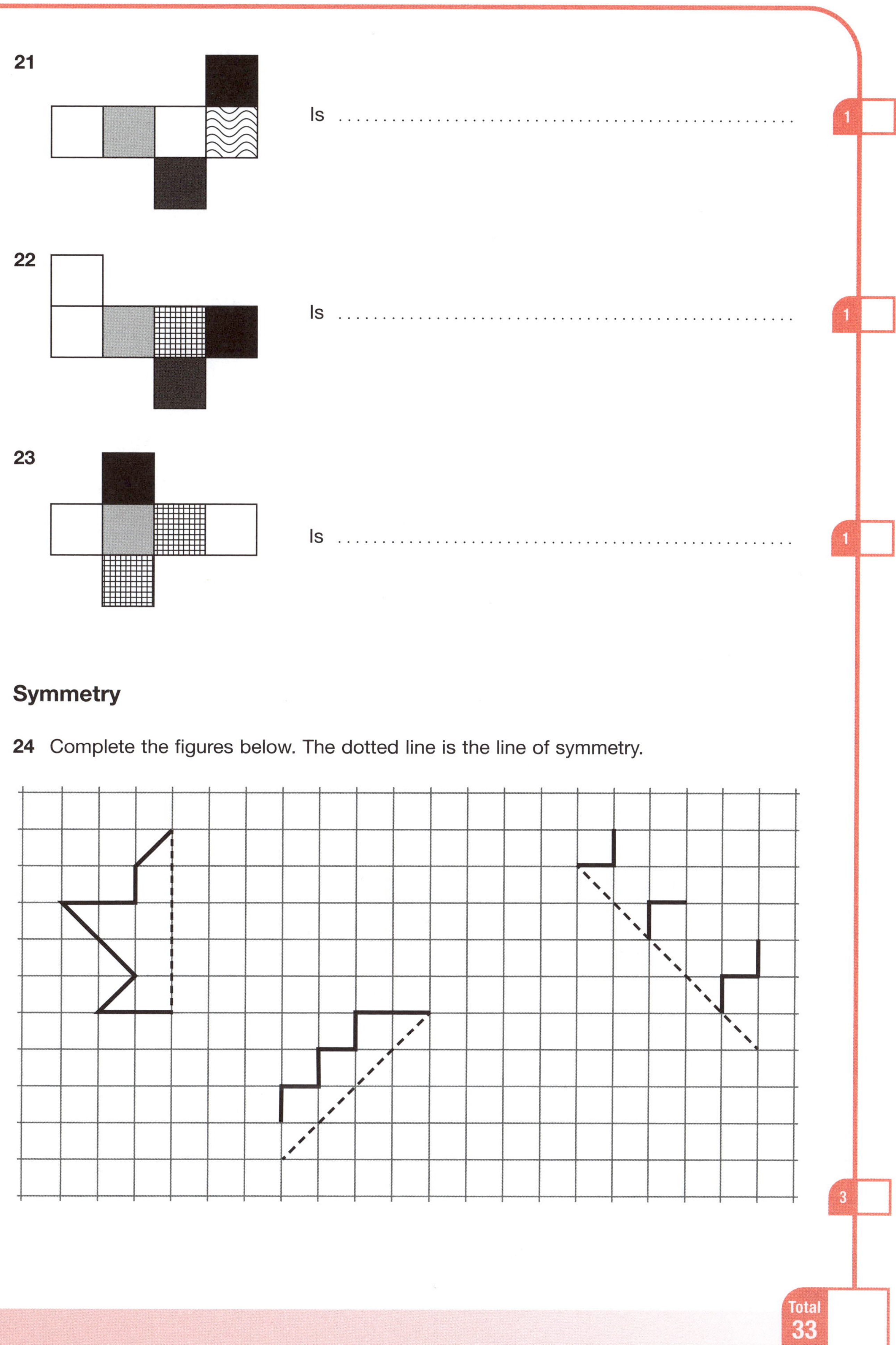

21
Is
1
22
Is
1
23
Is
1
Symmetry
24 Complete the figures below. The dotted line is the line of symmetry.
3
Total
33

Statistics and Probability

KEY SKILLS

Different Types of Graphs and Diagrams

A variety of graphs and diagrams are used to show information involving numbers. We will focus on three although there are many others you will come across later on in school.

- Venn diagrams are usually used when some values/people/things are present in more than one group, these values appear in the overlap of the groups.
- Bar charts are used where there is no overlap of values and the groups have no direct connection.
- Line graphs are used where there is no overlap of values and the groups have a connection.

Probability

Probability is the likelihood of something happening; first think of all the possible things that could happen and then how many ways of those ways fit.

To help us explain this we use the words event and outcome.

If an outcome is certain, its probability is 1. If an outcome is impossible, its probability is 0.

If an event is neither certain, nor impossible, then its probability is somewhere between zero and one and is often written as a fraction

For example, the probability of choosing a dog out of a group of 5 dogs and 4 cats.

5 dogs out of a total of 5 dogs and 4 cats.

5 out of (4 + 5) 5 out of 9.

We write this as a fraction (or decimal or percentage).

$$P(event) = \frac{successful\ outcomes}{total\ outcomes}$$

$$P(event) = \frac{successful\ outcomes}{successful\ outcomes + unsuccessful\ outcomes}$$

$$P(dog) = \frac{5}{5 + 4}$$

$$P(dog) = \frac{5}{9}$$

WORKED EXAMPLES

Here are the scores in a mental arithmetic test out of 20.

Name	Peter	Cressida	Petra	Greg	Helen
Score	17	16	18	16	17

There are two **modes**: what are they?

What is the **median**? What is the **range**? What is the **mean**?
The mode is the most common score. Two people scored 16 and two people scored 17.

To find the median of a set of numbers, list the numbers in order, smallest to largest (16, 16, 17, 17, 18). The median is the middle value of 17.

The range is the difference between the highest score and the lowest score (18 – 16 = 2).

To find the mean of a set of numbers, add the numbers together and then divide the total by the quantity of numbers in the group

(17 + 16 + 18 + 16 + 17 = 84; 84 ÷ 5 = 16.8).

30 mins

Statistics and Probability

Bar Charts

1 On the grid below, draw a bar chart to show the following information.

The number of cups of coffee sold at Buttercup Café last week:

Monday	90	Tuesday	110
Wednesday	70	Thursday	100
Friday	120	Saturday	140

Be careful to use a scale that will show this information accurately.
Write in your scale.

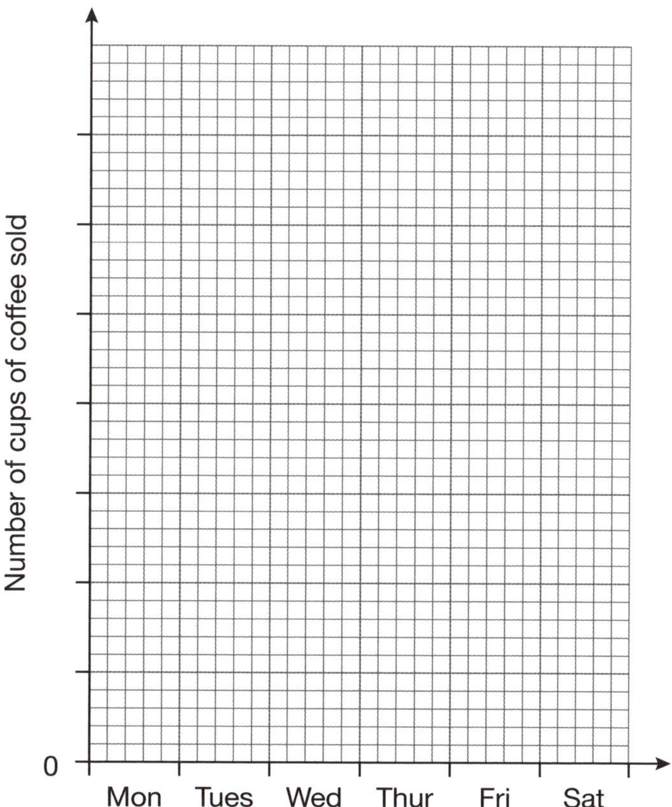

6

Learning Papers

Statistics and Probability

Line Graphs

2 Use the conversion graph to rewrite the road sign in kilometres.

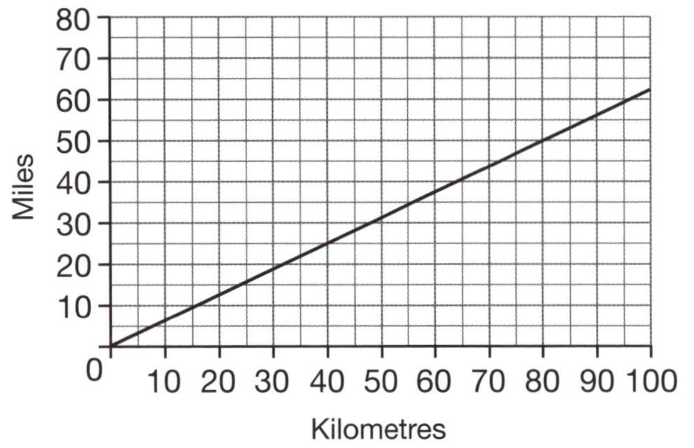

Darlington	25 miles
Newcastle	50 miles

Darlington ________ km

Newcastle ________ km

2

3 Approximately how many miles in 95 km? 1

4 Which is greater: 50 miles or 75 km? 1

Mean, Mode, Median and Range

Here are the scores in a science test out of 50.

Name	Kamala	Matt	Rashid	Jo	James
Score	42	15	26	31	26

5 What is the mode? 1

TOP TIP!

To find the median of a set of numbers, list them in order from smallest to largest. The median is the middle number. Not a problem if there is an odd number of values in the list, but if there is an even number you must find the average of the middle two numbers.

6 What is the median? 1

7 What is the range? 1

8 What is the mean? 1

Matt actually got 25 not 15.

9 What is the median now? 1

10 What is the range now? 1

Probability

There are six balls, numbered 1 to 6, in a bag. Write your answers as fractions.

11 What is the probability that I will draw out an even-numbered ball? 1

12 What is the probability that I will draw out the 5? 1

13 What is the probability that I will draw out an odd-numbered ball? 1

Venn Diagrams

14 Some children in a Youth Club made this Venn diagram to show which music they like.

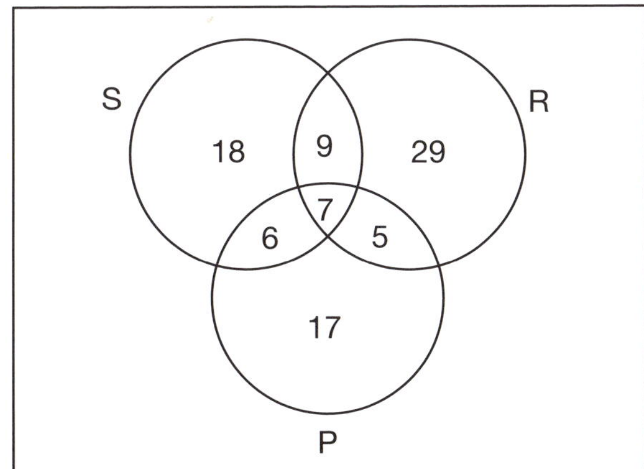

S = soul
R = rock
P = pop

.... children like soul, ... like rock and

.... like pop music. 3

15 The number of children who like both soul and rock is 1

16 How many like both soul and pop? 1

Total 24

Word and Logic Problems

KEY SKILLS

With word and logic problems you want to figure out a strategy to solve it.

First look for clues and relationships and prioritise your steps.

Key words to look for: **sum, total, double, halve, add.**

Questions you can ask yourself and steps you can take to help:

1. What do I have to find out?
2. How many pieces of information do I have?
3. Which is the most important?
4. Could I solve the problem if I took one piece of information away?
5. Do I need to prioritise the information to solve a problem?
6. Which information can I use first?
7. Where shall I start?
8. Do I just start at the top and work our way down, or do I start at the bottom and work up? Why not?
9. Which clue can I use next?
10. Ask questions such as 'If this ... then this will change ...'. 'What if . . . ?'
11. How am I going to solve the problem? What can I record to help me?
12. Review my work: Where am I? Where do I need to be? Is this working?
13. Check my answer meets all the criteria.

WORKED EXAMPLES

- Which number, when multiplied by 30, will give the same answer as 51 × 10?

  This is where it is good to know the factors, or even better, the prime factors of a number.

  $30 \times x = 51 \times 10$
  $3 \times 10 \times x = 3 \times 17 \times 103 \times 10 \times x =$
  $3 \times 10 \times 17$
  $x =$ **17**

- The perimeter of a rectangle is 40 cm. The length is 4 times the width.

  The length is .... cm and the width is .... cm.

  Here a picture is a good place to start, then some working out.

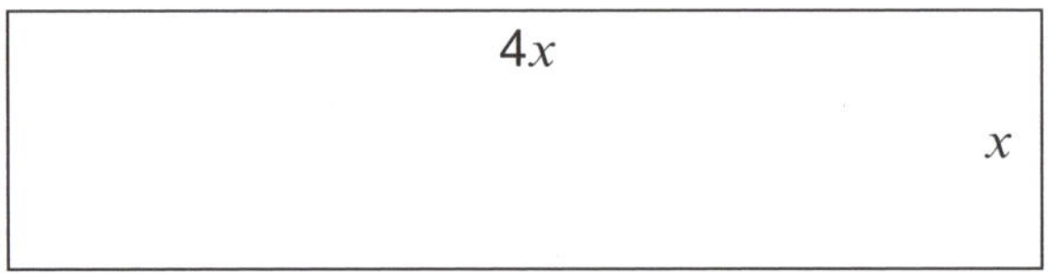

$4x + x + 4x + x = 40$

$10x = 40$

$x = 4\text{ cm}$ $4x = 16\text{ cm}$

The length is **16 cm**. The width is **4 cm**.

30 mins

Word Problems

1 How many comics, costing £1.75 each, can be bought for £15.00? 1

2 How many packets, each holding 125 g, can be filled from a case holding 3 kg?

.... 1

3 Jenny bought 7 metres of material. She gave the assistant £20.00 and received £2.57 change.

What was the price of the material per metre? 1

4 Twelve toys were bought for £1.25 each and sold for £1.60 each. What was the total profit? 1

5 Add the greatest value to the smallest.

£$\frac{1}{2}$ £0.55 27 × 2p £$\frac{13}{25}$ £1.00 – 49p 1

6 A coil of rope was divided into 7 equal sections, each 17.5 metres long. If there were 3.25 m left, how long was the rope? 1

7 A greenhouse can be bought by paying a deposit of £45, and then 12 monthly payments of £37.50.

What would be the total cost of the greenhouse? 1

8 Horsforth United had 5000 spectators to watch their game this week. Each stand seats 870.

What is the fewest number of stands required for this crowd? 1

Logic Problems

9 What is the nearest number to 1000, but smaller than 1000, into which 38 will divide with no remainder?

.... 1

TOP TIP!

To find the number halfway between two numbers, add the 2 numbers together and then divide by 2.

For example: 13 and 21

$$\frac{13 + 21}{2} = \frac{34}{2} = 17$$

10 What number is halfway between 37 and 111? 1

Three buses leave the bus station at 7 a.m. Service A runs every 5 minutes. Service B runs every 15 minutes. Service C runs every 12 minutes.

11 At what time will all three services again start from the bus station at the same time? 1

12 25 telegraph posts are spaced equally along the side of a road. If there is 85 m between each pair of posts, how long is that stretch of road in metres? 1

The population of Grangetown is 11 552. The men and children together number 8763, and the men and women total 5874.

13 How many women are there? 1

14 There are .... children. 1

15 How many men are there? 1

16 Thirty-six posts were spaced evenly along a road that was 1.575 km long. What was the distance in metres between each pair of posts? 1

17 The average of 4 numbers is $10\frac{1}{2}$.

If the average of 3 of them is 9, what is the 4th number? 1

18 $\frac{3}{4}$ of a sum of money is £1.80. What is $\frac{1}{3}$ of it? 1

19 In a school there were a total of 476 pupils and teachers.

The girls + the teachers = 241

The boys + the teachers = 258

There were .... teachers, ... boys and .... girls. 3

The products of the following calculations are either odd or even.

Answer each question as either ODD or EVEN.

20 84 × 36 is an .... number. 1

21 163 × 297 is an .... number. 1

22 729 × 1468 is an .... number. 1

23 292 × 36 × 52 is an .... number. 1

Total 25

Word and Logic Problems

Curveball Questions 1

20 mins

1 Choose from numbers 1 – 12 to complete the top row and first column of the multiplication grid. One has been done for you. Numbers can only be used once.

x			1			
		12				
						56
		8		12		
			9		90	
	60					40

Now add all the numbers in your top row. What is the total? 12

2 Using the tiles below, create a path from each 3D shape to its corresponding number of edges. The paths cannot cross and no square in the grid can be left blank.

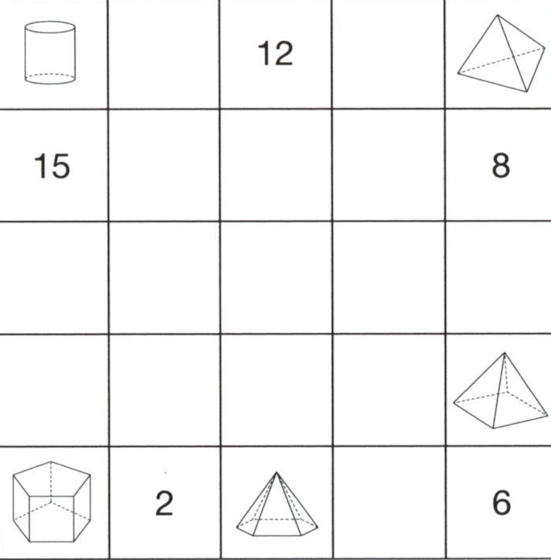

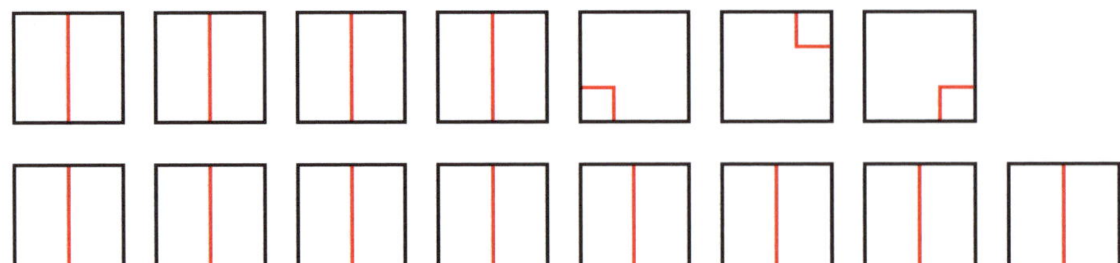

Which shape's path has more than one corner? 6

Total 18

Mixed Papers

Mixed Paper 1

40 mins

1 Write in figures: one hundred and two thousand and twenty-one. 1

2 Which of the numbers in the oval is 2^2? 1

3 Which of the numbers in the oval is 5^2? 1

4 Which of the numbers in the oval is 3^2? 1

5 Which of the numbers in the oval is 6^2? 1

TOP TIP!

Some quick ways to find percentages: find 10% by dividing by 10, then 1% by dividing by 10 again; find 50% by dividing by 2 and 5% by halving 10%

For example, £234: 10% = £23.40, 1% = £2.34, 50% = £117, 5% = £11.70.

Since 66% = 50% + 10% + 5% + 1%, 66% of £234 = £117 + £23.40 + £11.70 + £2.40 = £154.44

6 VAT (Value Added Tax) is charged at 20% on some goods. This means that a £100.00 item would have a tax of £20 added to its cost.

Complete the table.

Price before VAT	VAT	Total cost
£180.00	....	....
£420.00	....	....
£340.00	....	....

6

Mixed Papers

Mixed Paper 1

7 Put these numbers in order, smallest first. 0.707 0.78 0.708 0.7 0.77

.... 5

8 In a school 6 out of every 11 children are girls.

If there are 407 children in the school, there are:

.... boys and .... girls. 2

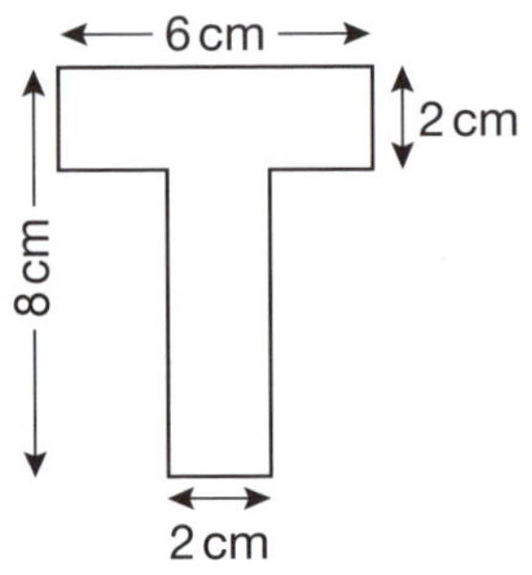

9 What is the area of the shape? .... cm^2 1

10 What is the perimeter of the shape? .... cm 1

Write the times which are a quarter of an hour before the following times.

11 22:00 1

12 11:05 1

13 13:10 1

14 Complete the drawings below using the line of symmetry marked by the dashes.

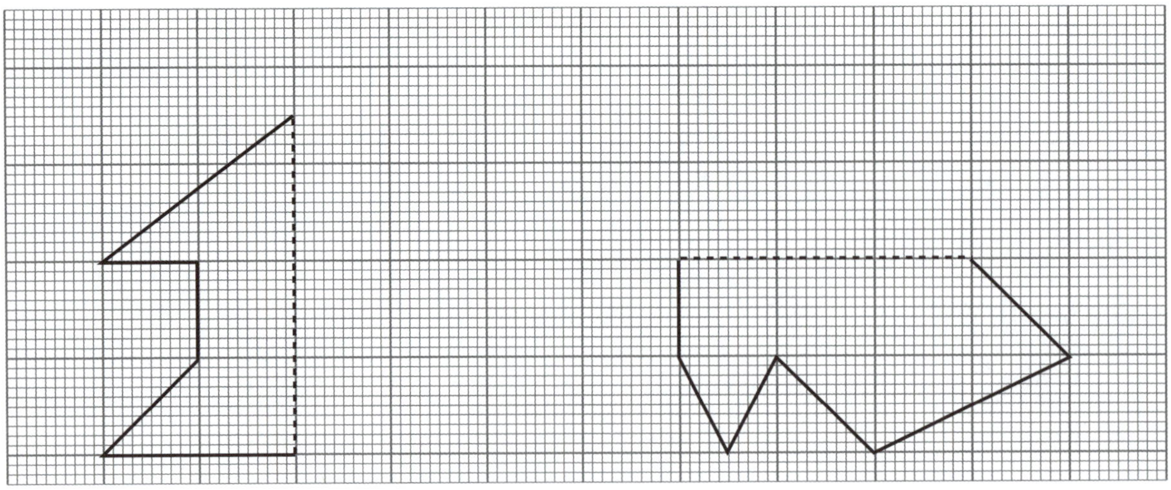

2

We asked 144 children at our school how they spent their holiday. When we got their answers, we made this pie chart.

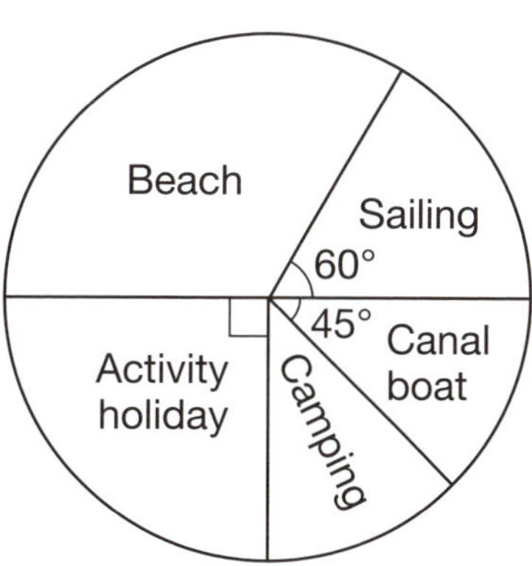

15 How many children went to the beach? 1

16 How many went sailing? 1

17 The number of children who went on an Activity holiday was 1

18 How many went camping? 1

19 How many went canal boating? 1

Ted has £98 and Zac has £64.

20 How much must Ted give to Zac so that they each have the same amount? 1

21 Angle x = ... 1

22 Angle $2x$ = ... 1

23 Angle a = ... 1

24 Angle b = ... 1

25 What would be the approximate cost of 13 films at £4.98 each (to the nearest £)? 1

26 Write down the numbers that will come out of this machine. 4

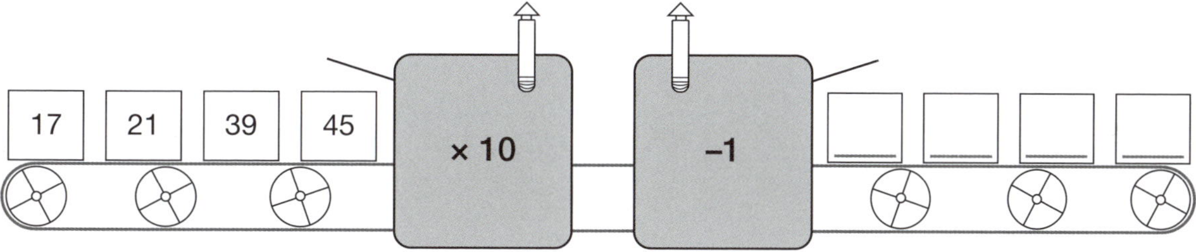

Total 40

Mixed Paper 2

Mixed Papers

Mixed Paper 2

40 mins

1 Write these numbers to the nearest 100.

298 847 503 1074

.... 4

quotient the answer if you divide one number by another, for example the quotient of 12 ÷ 4 is 3

2 Work out these, and then write them out in order, from highest to lowest **quotient**.

$7\overline{)315}$ $8\overline{)392}$ $7\overline{)329}$ $9\overline{)387}$

.... 4

Which numbers are the arrows pointing to on this number line?

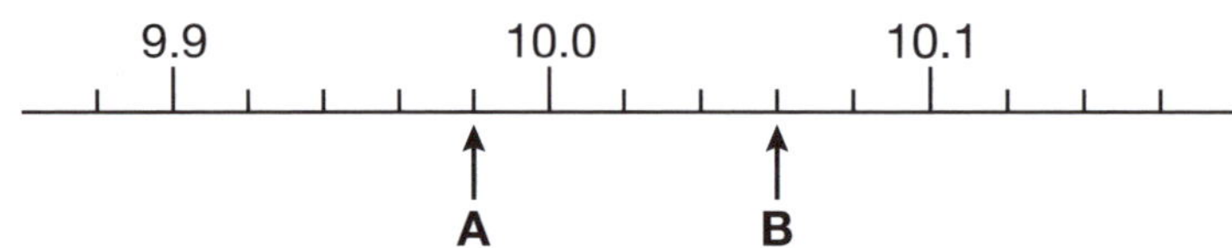

3 Arrow A points to 1

4 Arrow B points to 1

5 Arrange these fractions in order, largest first.

$\frac{7}{12}$ $\frac{3}{8}$ $\frac{3}{4}$ $\frac{11}{24}$ $\frac{5}{6}$

.... 5

Some game cards are shared between Thomas and Matthew in the ratio of 5 : 4.

6 If Matthew receives 16 Thomas will get 1

7 If they shared the same cards equally (not in 5 : 4) Matthew would receive 1

8 How many metres must be added to 1.35 km to make 4 km? 1

Here is Pavel's temperature chart when he was ill.

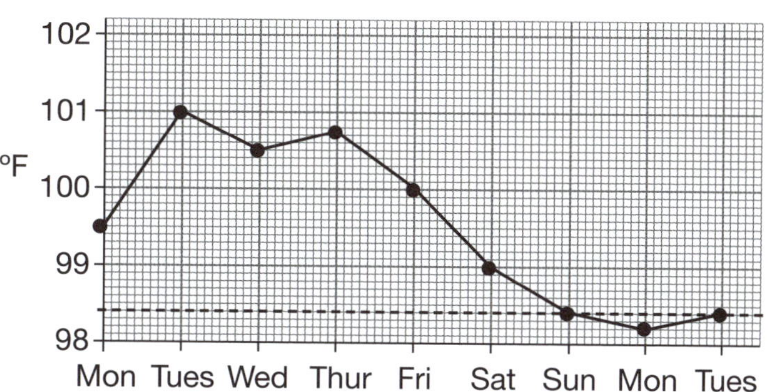

The dotted line shows the normal temperature of a person.

9 On how many days was his temperature above normal? 1

10 On how many days was his temperature below normal? 1

11 On which day do you think he was most ill? 1

12 On which day do you think he started getting better? 1

13 What is a person's normal temperature? 1

A fair coin is tossed at the start of a game. Underline the correct answer to each question.

14 What is the probability of getting heads?

$\frac{2}{3}$ $\frac{4}{5}$ $\frac{1}{2}$ $\frac{3}{4}$ 1

15 What is the probability of getting tails?

$\frac{2}{3}$ $\frac{4}{5}$ $\frac{1}{2}$ $\frac{3}{4}$ 1

Mixed Paper 2

Mixed Papers

Mixed Paper 2

TOP TIP!

There are 12 months in a year, so you can use **mixed numbers**.

4 years 5 months = $4\frac{5}{12}$ years.

16 Look at the table.

The children's ages add up to .... years .... months. 2

	Years	Months
Tony is	10	8
Claire is	9	6
Abdel is	11	4
Mandy is	10	2

17 What is the mean age of the four children? .... years .... months 2

The big hand of a clock is at 12 and the small hand is not. If the little hand moves in a clockwise direction, what time is it when the angle between the two hands is:

18 180°? .... o'clock

19 30°? .... o'clock

20 120°? .... o'clock

21 60°? .... o'clock

22 150°? .... o'clock 5

Your task is to guide the robot along the white squares on the plan.
The robot starts and finishes on one of the squares marked A, B, C, D or E.
It can only move FORWARD, turn RIGHT 90° and turn LEFT 90°.

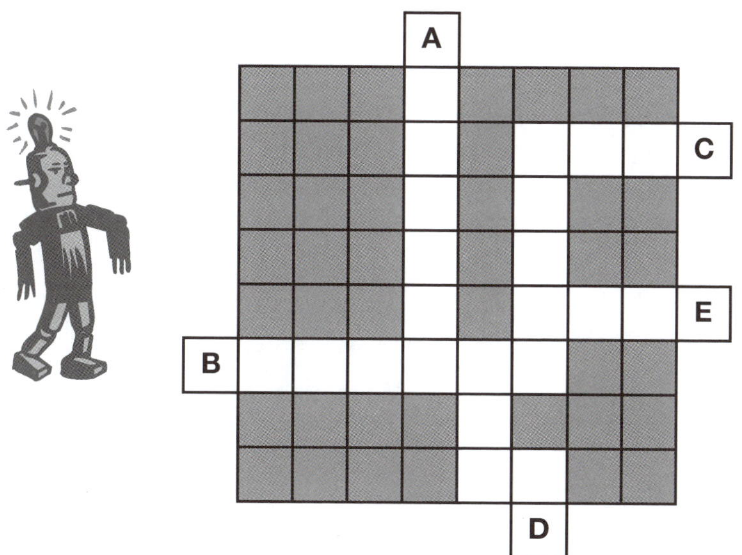

Complete these instructions to guide the robot along the white squares.

23 From A to B: FORWARD 6, RIGHT 90°, ... 1

24 From B to C: FORWARD 6, ... , FORWARD 4, RIGHT 90°, FORWARD 3. 1

25 From C to E: FORWARD 3, LEFT 90°, ... , LEFT 90°, FORWARD 3. 1

26 From D to B: FORWARD 1, LEFT 90°, FORWARD 1, ... , ... , LEFT 90°, FORWARD 5. 1

Mr Pin paid £7.05 for 1.5 metres of material.

27 What was the cost per metre? 1

28 How much would 3.5 m cost? 1

Total 40

Mixed Paper 2

Mixed Paper 3

Mixed Papers

Mixed Paper 3

40 mins

1 What is the smallest number into which 6, 8, 10 and 12 will all divide without remainder? 1

2 8 − 1.127 = ... 1

3 47.625 ÷ 2.5 = ... 1

4 Make 999 ten times as large. 1

5 Write these fractions as decimals.

$4\frac{1}{2}$ $7\frac{1}{10}$ $3\frac{9}{100}$ 3

6 A number multiplied by itself is 16. What is the number? 1

7 What amount must be added to 178.5 g to make 1 kg? .... g 1

8 Plot the following coordinates on the chart and join them in the order that you plot them.

(−3, −2) (−3, 3) (−1, 1) (1, 3) (1, −2)

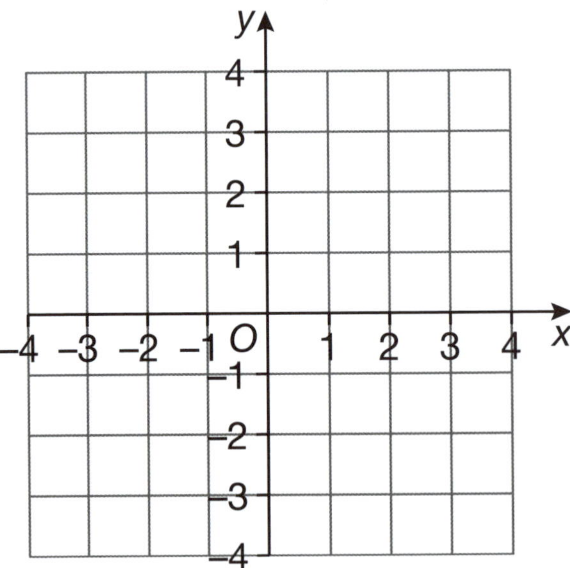

5

TOP TIP!

To find the mean of a set of numbers, add the numbers together and then divide the total by the quantity of numbers in the group.

What is the average (mean) of the following numbers?

9 7 4 6 8 5 1

10 3 2 7 1

11 4 4 6 2 1

A bag contains 4 grey balls and 3 white balls. Underline the correct answer to each question.

12 What is the probability of picking a white ball?

$\frac{3}{4}$ $\frac{3}{5}$ $\frac{3}{6}$ $\frac{3}{7}$ $\frac{3}{8}$

13 What is the probability of picking a grey ball?

0 $\frac{1}{2}$ $\frac{4}{7}$ $\frac{3}{7}$ $\frac{3}{4}$

14 What is the probability of picking a black ball?

0 $\frac{1}{2}$ $\frac{4}{7}$ $\frac{3}{7}$ $\frac{3}{4}$ 3

15 By how much is the product of 27 and 13 greater than their sum? 1

Your task is to guide the robot along the white squares on the plan.
It starts and finishes on one of the squares marked A, B, C, D or E.
It can only move FORWARD, turn RIGHT 90° and turn LEFT 90°.

Complete these instructions to guide the robot along the white squares.

16 From A to B:

FORWARD 2, ..., FORWARD 1, RIGHT 90°, FORWARD 3,

LEFT 90°, ..., RIGHT 90°, FORWARD 4 2

17 From B to C:

FORWARD 4, LEFT 90°, FORWARD 1, RIGHT 90°, ..., LEFT 90°,

FORWARD 3 ...., FORWARD 1, RIGHT 90°, FORWARD 2 2

18 From C to D:

FORWARD 2, LEFT 90°, FORWARD 1, RIGHT 90°, FORWARD 3, LEFT 90°,

FORWARD 1, ..., ..., LEFT 90°, FORWARD 1, RIGHT 90°, FORWARD 2 2

Find the following:

19 The factors of 12 are 1, 2, ..., ..., ... and 1

20 The factors of 20 are 1, ..., ..., ..., ... and

.... 1

21 The factors of 15 are ...., ..., ... and ....

22 The numbers that are factors of both 12 and 20 are 1, ... and ....

23 The numbers that are factors of both 12 and 15 are 1 and ....

24 The numbers that are factors of both 20 and 15 are 1 and ....

25 Now fill in the lengths of the sides of the box using these answers.

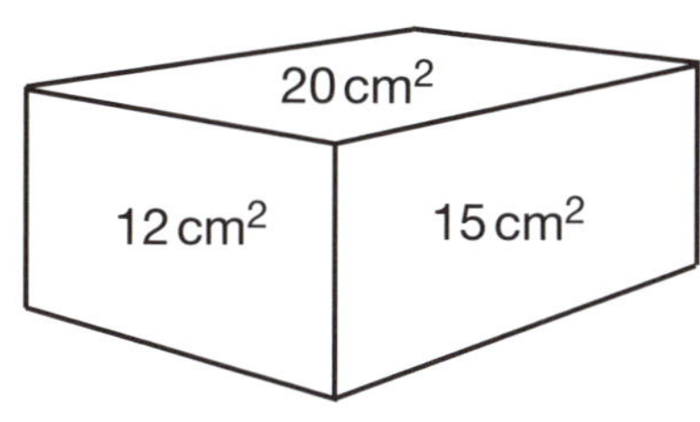

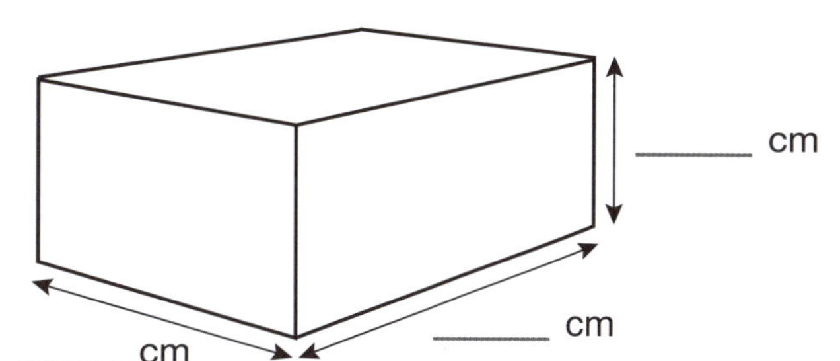

1
1
1
1
3

Mixed Paper 3

State whether the following statements are TRUE or FALSE.

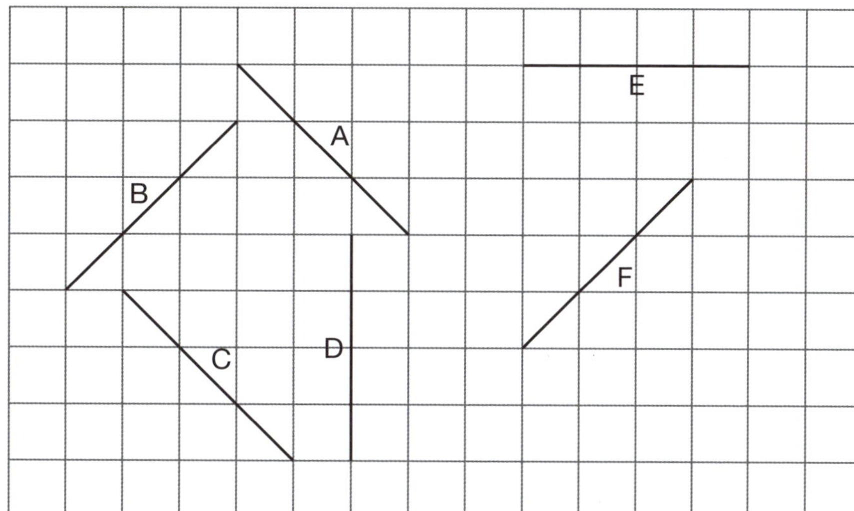

26 Line B is parallel to line A. ....

27 Line C is perpendicular to line F. ....

28 Line E is a horizontal line. ....

29 Line D is a vertical line. ....

4

Total 40

Mixed Paper 4

40 mins

1 5 is a prime factor of 2475.

What are the other two prime factors? .... and 2

TOP TIP!

To add fractions together, first find equivalent fractions so that the denominators are the same.

2 $7\frac{7}{8} + 5\frac{13}{16} =$ 1

3 $7\frac{1}{5} - 3\frac{11}{15} =$ 1

£1 = 1.46 US dollars
£1 = 119 Kenyan shillings
£1 = 1.16 euros

4 How many US dollars do you get for £10? 1

5 How many Kenyan shillings do you get for £100? 1

6 How many euros do you get for £1000? 1

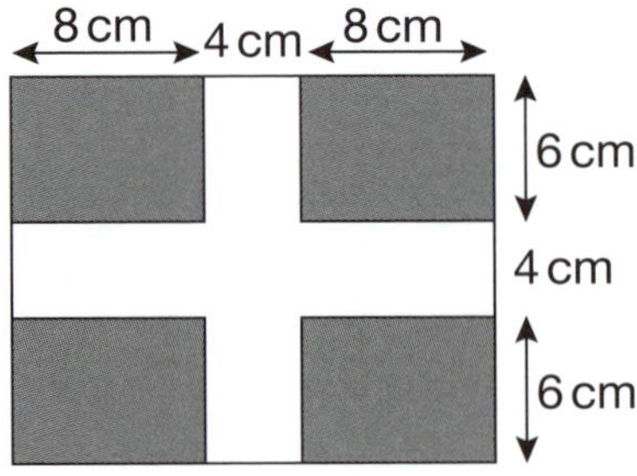

7 What is the total area of the flag? 1

8 What is the area of the cross? 1

9 What is the area of the grey area? 1

10 What is the perimeter of the flag? 1

11 What is the perimeter of the cross? 1

Give the most appropriate metric unit to measure:

12 the distance from Earth to the Sun. 1

13 the amount of petrol in a car. 1

14 the weight of a train. 1

15 the thickness of this book. 1

Here are three shaded cubes.

A B C

Which cube has the following nets? Choose between A, B, C or none.

16

Is 1

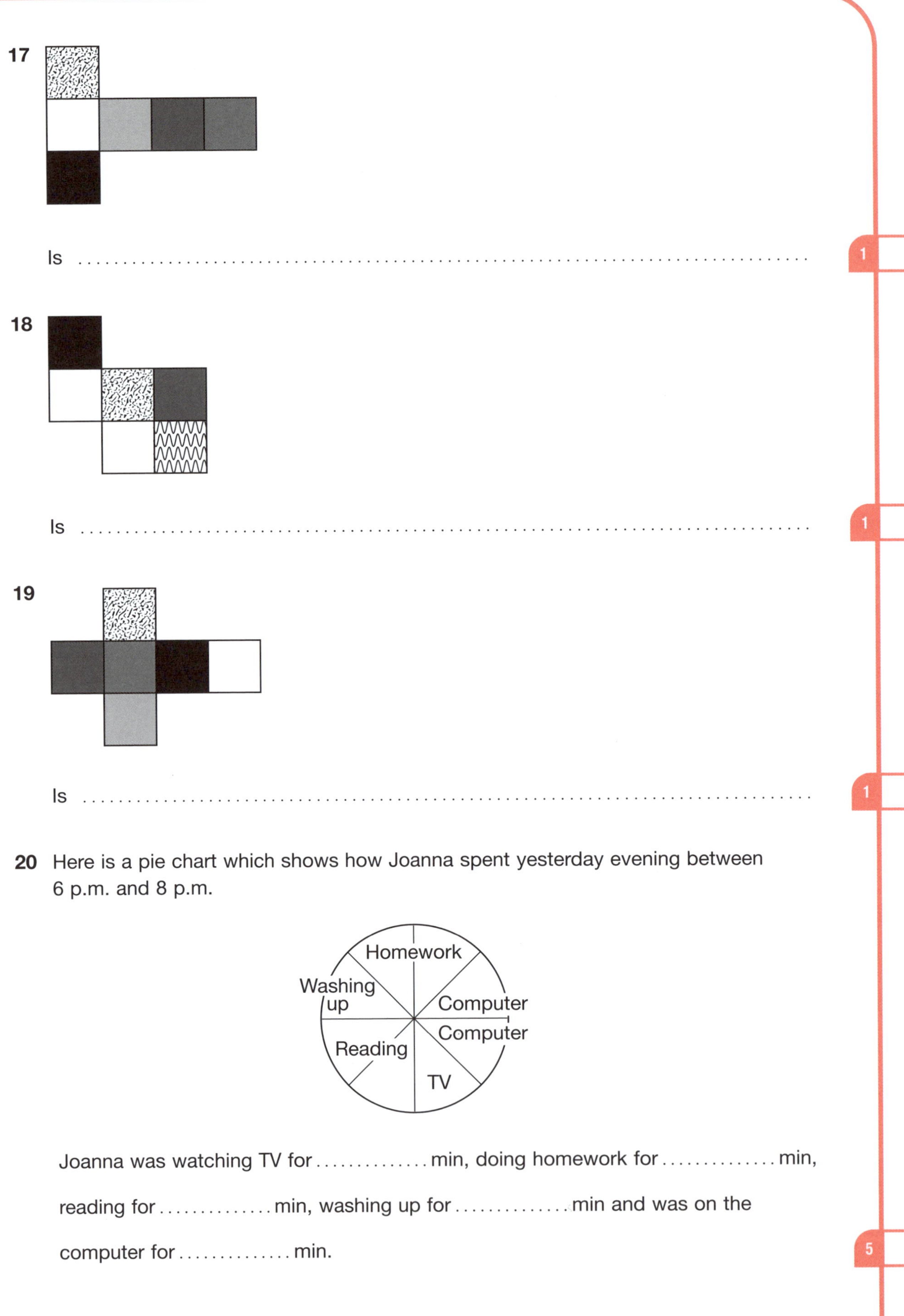

17

Is 1

18

Is 1

19

Is 1

20 Here is a pie chart which shows how Joanna spent yesterday evening between 6 p.m. and 8 p.m.

Joanna was watching TV for .... min, doing homework for .... min,

reading for .... min, washing up for .... min and was on the

computer for .... min. 5

21–22 John used this decision tree to sort paint. What is missing from the tree? Fill in the gaps.

2

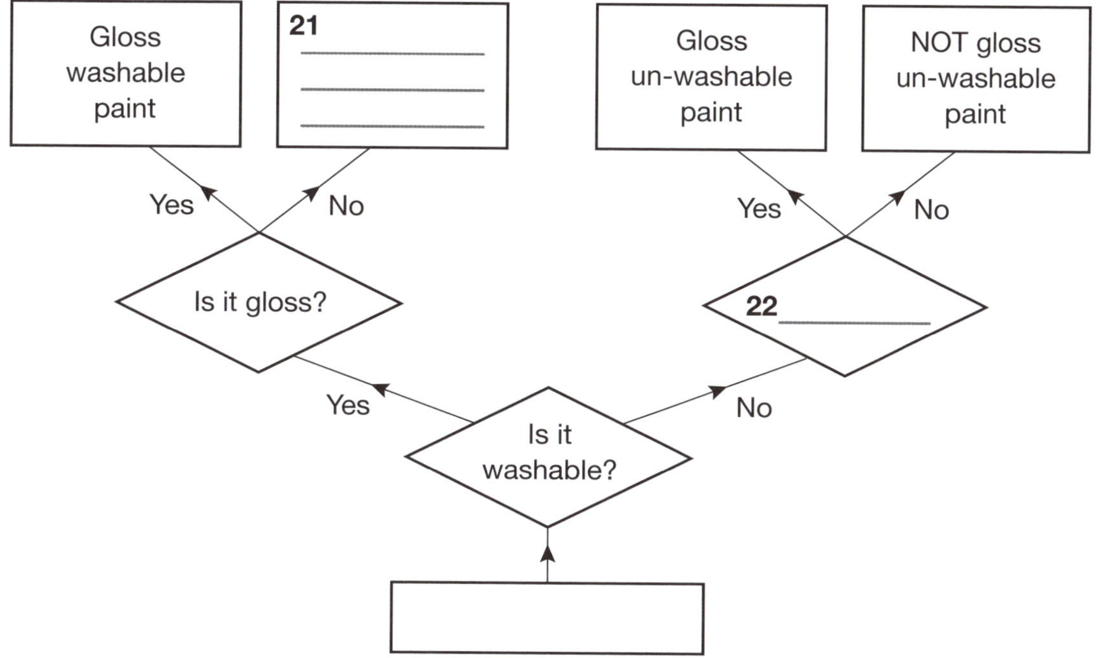

The bar chart below shows the marks in Mathematics for Class 8.

$\frac{2}{5}$ of those who received between 81 and 90 were girls.

$\frac{3}{4}$ of those who received between 71 and 80 were boys.

$\frac{1}{2}$ of those who received between 61 and 70 were girls.

$\frac{1}{3}$ of those who received between 51 and 60 were girls.

$\frac{1}{2}$ of those who received between 41 and 50 were boys.

1 boy gained over 90 marks.

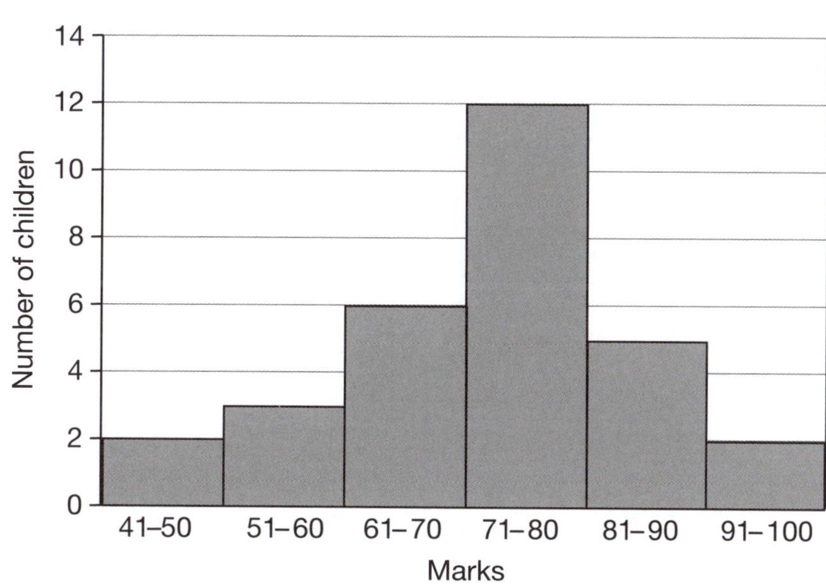

Mixed Paper 4

23 How many children took the test? 1

24 How many girls got over 90 marks? 1

25 How many boys received between 61 and 70 marks? 1

26 How many girls received between 41 and 50 marks? 1

27 In the 71 to 80 mark range, how many were girls? 1

28 How many boys received between 51 and 60 marks? 1

29 Convert this recipe for pasta from imperial to metric units (to the nearest 5g). 3
Use the approximation: 1 oz = 25g

Ingredient	Imperial	Metic
Plain flour	5 oz	
Semolina flour	12 oz	
Eggs	11 eggs	

Here is a box 20 cm long, 10 cm wide, and 8 cm high.

A ribbon is placed round the box, once lengthwise, and once round the width.

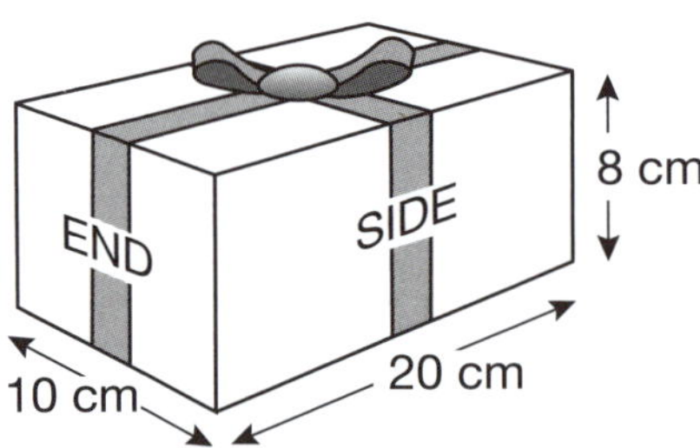

30 What is the perimeter of the side of the box? 1

31 What is the perimeter of the end of the box? 1

32 What is the perimeter of the base of the box? 1

33 If I allow 35 cm for the bow, how much ribbon will I need? 1

Total 40

Curveball Questions 2

15 mins

1 Each of the four balance scales are perfectly balanced.

All the balls of the same colour (black, white, grey or striped) have identical weights.
No two different coloured balls weigh the same.

What is the colour of the ball with the question mark? 5

Complete the table using the numbers below.
Each column, row and diagonal add up to the same number.

What is the value of the question mark? ....

40		
		70
	?	

10, 40, 20, 30 80, 90, 60, 50, 70 5

Total 10

Test Paper 1

60 mins

TOP TIP!

Use your time wisely: answer all the questions you know you can do quicky first. Mark the other questions: with a "T" if you think it will take a long time, and a "?" if you don't know how to do it. Then do all the "T" questions, followed by the "?" questions.

Write each of these values in decimal form.

1 7 thousandths 1

2 259 tens 1

3 14 hundredths 1

4 Put a circle around the numbers which are not **prime numbers**.

3 13 23 33 43 53 63 2

$5 \times 5 = 5^2$ $2 \times 2 \times 2 = 2^3$. Now write the following in the same way.

5 $4 \times 4 \times 4 \times 4 =$ 1

6 $11 \times 11 \times 11 \times 11 \times 11 =$ 1

7 What number is $1 \times 1 \times 1 \times 1 \times 1 \times 1$? 1

8 How many fifths are there in $12\frac{4}{5}$? 1

There are 420 children in a school. 45% of the pupils are boys.

9 How many boys are there? 1

10 If $\frac{5}{12}$ of the contents of a box weigh 20 kg, what is the weight of all the contents?

.... 1

11 What would $\frac{1}{8}$ of the contents weigh? 1

In the end-of-term tests Zanna got the following marks.

Mathematics $\frac{54}{75}$

English $\frac{48}{60}$

History $\frac{27}{40}$

French $\frac{25}{40}$

Geography $\frac{39}{50}$

Art $\frac{15}{20}$

12 Her best subject was 1

13 2nd was 1

14 3rd was 1

15 4th was 1

16 5th was 1

17 6th was 1

$\frac{2}{3}$ of a sum of money is 48p.

18 What is $\frac{5}{8}$ of the sum of money? 1

£9.00 is shared between Amanda, Anita and Claire in the ratio of 8:5:2.

19 Amanda receives 1

20 Anita receives 1

21 Claire receives 1

Test Paper 1

Test Papers

Test Paper 1

Insert signs to make the following correct.

22 5 .... 5 .... 1 = 13 .... 12 3

23 (3 .... 2) .... 5 = 50 .... 2 3

Find the area of these triangles. Scale: 1 square = 1 cm^2

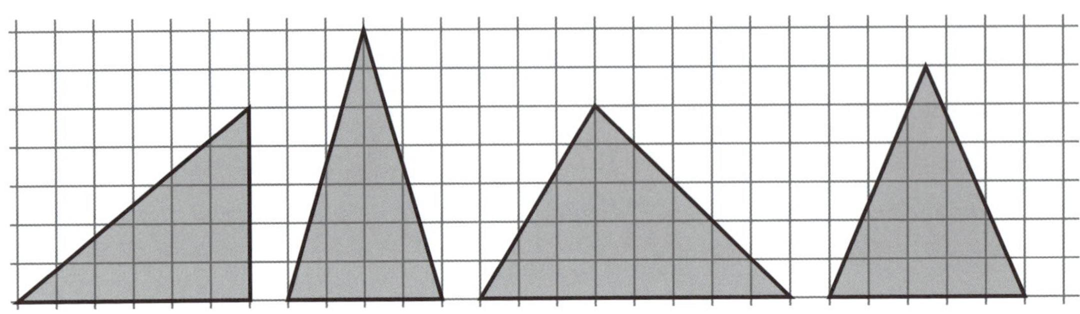

24 .... **25** .... **26** **27** 4

Convert the following lengths to kilometres.

28 1357 m = ... 1

29 12 986 m = ... 1

30 456 m = ... 1

31 Find the area of a square whose perimeter is 12 cm. 1

	Train A	Train B	Train C	Train D
Westbury	08:11	09:20	18:09	20:09
Trowbridge	08:19	09:30	17:58	20:04
Bath	08:45	09:54	17:23	19:31
Bristol	09:00	10:11	17:05	19:17

32 How long does the slowest train take to do the entire journey? 1

33 If I live in Westbury, and want to be in Bath before 9 a.m., on which train must I travel? 1

34 How long does the 19:31 from Bath take to travel to Westbury? 1

35 When should the 17:23 from Bath arrive in Westbury? 1

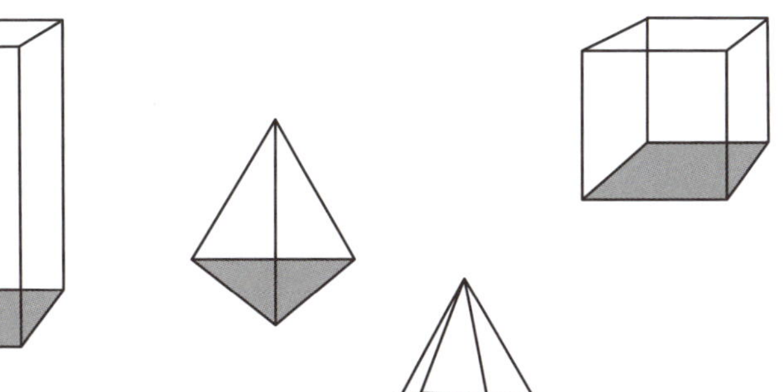

36 Complete the table.

Name of solid	Number of faces	Number of vertices	Number of edges
Triangular-based pyramid			
Square-based pyramid			
Cube			

9

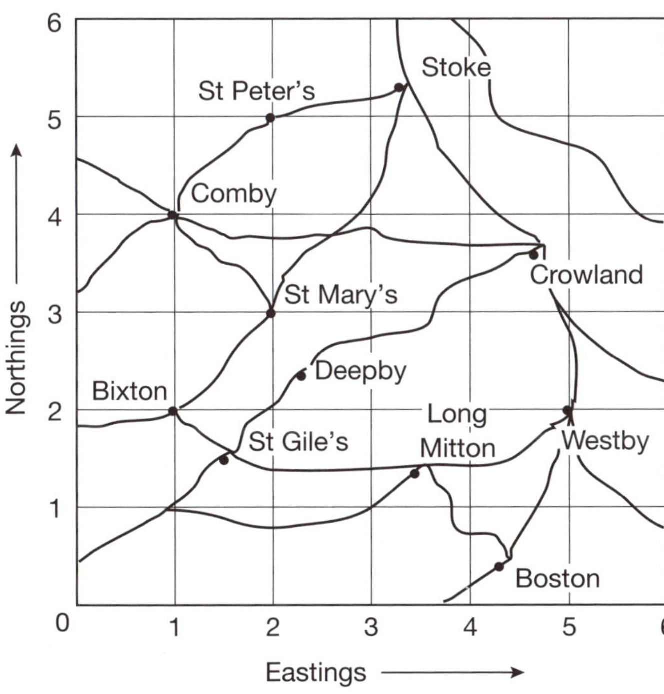

This map is covered with a grid, the lines of which are numbered 0–6 for eastings and 0–6 for northings. The position of towns is found by giving their coordinates, for example Bixton is (1, 2).

Some of the towns are not situated on the lines, but are inside the squares.

When this is so, the coordinates of the bottom left-hand corner of the square are given, for example Deepby is (2, 2).

Scale: A side of a small square represents 10 km. Name the towns which are at the following positions.

Test Paper 1

Test Papers

Test Paper 1

37 (3, 1) 1

38 (4, 0) 1

Give the coordinates for the following towns.

39 Comby (..............,..............) 1

40 Stoke (..............,..............) 1

Approximately, how far is it, as the crow flies (in a straight line), from:

41 St Gile's to Long Mitton? 1

42 Bixton to Westby? 1

Complete the figures below. The dotted line is the line of symmetry.

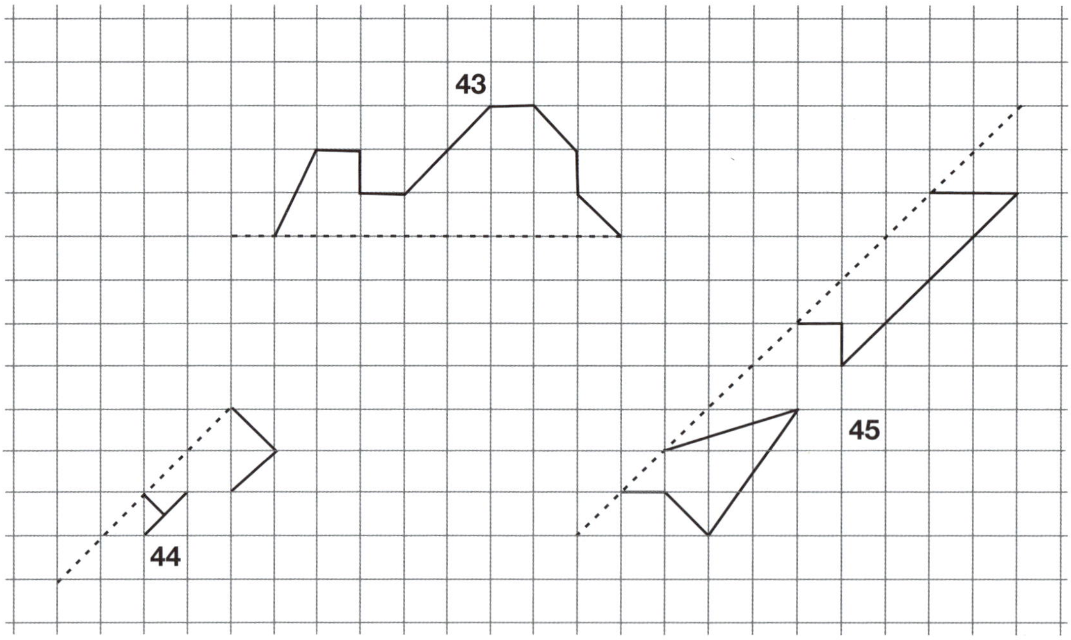

43

44

45

3

46 On the grid below draw a bar chart to show the information in the table.

Be careful to use a scale which will show this information accurately. Write in your scale.

Shop	Cameras sold
A	225
B	75
C	150
D	175
E	300
F	125
G	200

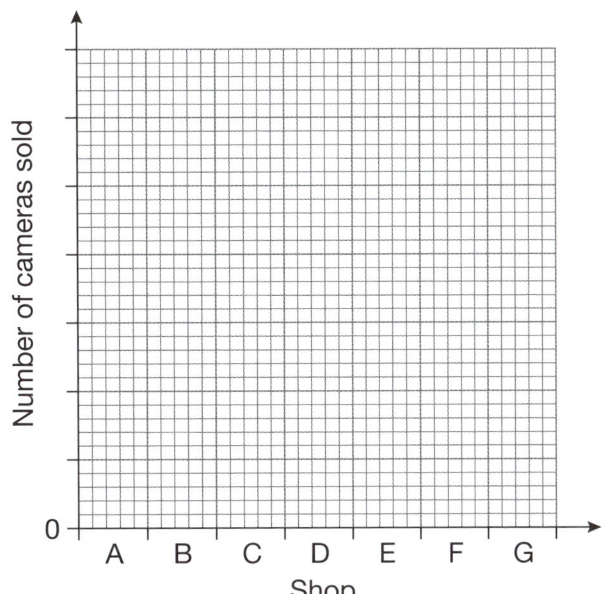

7

47 The average of 6 numbers is 4.

If one of the numbers is 2, what is the average of the other 5 numbers? 1

We asked 72 children to name their favourite colour.

We made this pie chart.

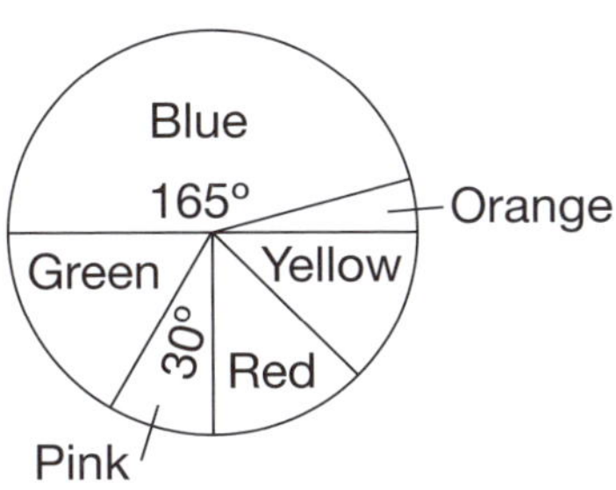

48 How many children prefer green? 1

49 How many children prefer blue? 1

50 How many prefer orange? 1

51 How many like red best 1

52 The number of children who prefer pink is 1

A fair dice numbered 1 to 6 is rolled at the start of a game. Underline the correct answer to each question.

53 What is the probability of getting a 6? 1

$\frac{2}{3}$ $\frac{1}{6}$ $\frac{1}{2}$ $\frac{3}{4}$

54 What is the probability of getting a 5? 1

$\frac{1}{3}$ $\frac{1}{4}$ $\frac{1}{5}$ $\frac{1}{6}$

55 What is the probability of getting a 2 or a 3? 1

$\frac{1}{6}$ $\frac{1}{3}$ $\frac{1}{2}$ $\frac{2}{3}$

There are 24 children in our class. This Venn diagram shows how many of us belong to the Cycling Club (C) and how many of us belong to the Swimming Club (S).

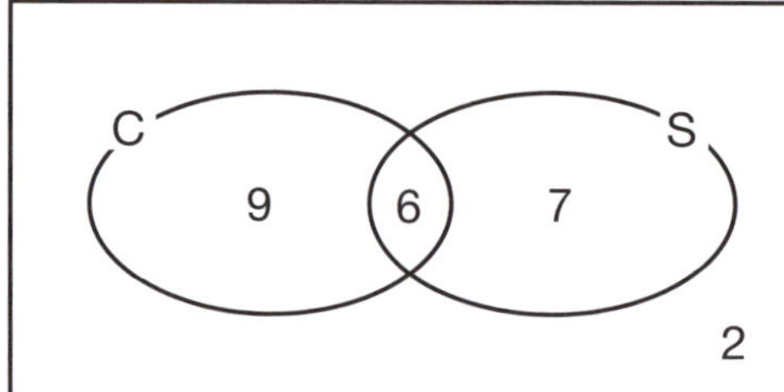

56 How many belong to the Cycling Club? ....

57 How many belong to the Swimming Club? ....

58 How many belong to both clubs? ....

59 How many belong to neither club? ....

60 How many belong to one club only? ....

61 How many tiles, each 50 cm × 50 cm, would be needed to cover a floor

5 metres × 4 metres? 1

Total 80

Test Paper 2

60 mins

TOP TIP!

Before you start the test paper make sure you have enough time available to complete it. When you start, the first thing to do is to look through all the questions so you know how long the paper is and check what the last page looks like. If you finish early, go back and check your answers.

1 Would you estimate the number of children in a class to the nearest

10, 100, 1000? 1

2 Would you estimate the number of people at a Premier League football game to the

nearest 10, 1 000, 10 000 or 1 000 000? 1

3 Underline the prime factors of 21.

2 3 4 5 6 7 8 2

4 How many times can 34 be subtracted from 986? 1

5 In the library there are 200 books. 58 of them are non-fiction. What percentage of

the books are non-fiction? 2

Which numbers are the arrows pointing to on this number line?

0.80 0.81 0.82

C B A

6 Arrow A points to 1

7 Arrow B points to 1

8 Arrow C points to 1

Test Paper 2

Divide these numbers by 1000.

9 374 1

10 14.8 1

11 2.55 1

Write these fractions in decimal form.

12 $3\frac{1}{8}$ 1

13 $4\frac{1}{20}$ 1

14 $7\frac{5}{8}$ 1

15 $9\frac{3}{40}$ 1

16 Complete this table.

✤ = a + 3

a		1		3
✤	3		5	

4

Fill in the next two numbers in each line.

17 95 89 84 80 2

18 89 77 67 59 2

19 31 33 36 40 2

20 144 121 100 81 2

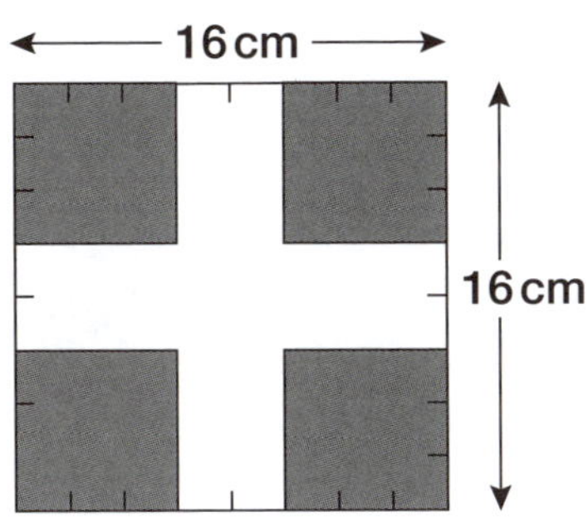

21 The area of the flag is ....

22 The area of the cross is ....

23 The shaded part has an area of ....

24 The perimeter of the flag is ....

28 The perimeter of the cross is ....

Suggest the best imperial unit to measure:

26 the distance from London to New York. ....

27 the amount of water in a jug. ....

28 the weight of a pencil. ....

29 the height of a person. ....

30 Fill in the gaps.

	Length	Width	Perimeter
Rectangle 1	18 cm		40 cm
Rectangle 2		3 cm	30 cm
Rectangle 3	9 cm	4 cm	
Square	6 cm		

Test Paper 2

Using this world time chart answer the following questions.

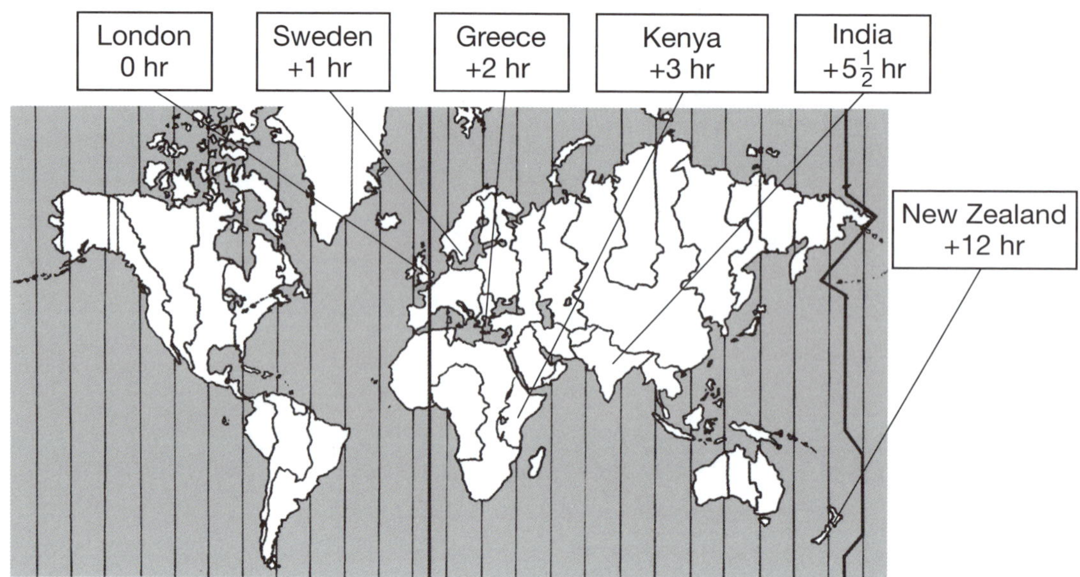

31 When it is 10:00 a.m. in London, what time is it in New Zealand? 1

32 When it is 9:00 a.m. in London, what time is it in India? 1

33 When it is 3:30 p.m. in Greece, what time is it in London? 1

34 When it is 1:15 p.m. in Sweden, what time is it in London? 1

35 If I made a telephone call from Kenya to India
at 3:00 p.m., what time would it be in India? 1

36

NW N NE
W E
SW S SE

You start facing	turn through	clockwise/ anticlockwise	you are now facing
W	135°	anticlockwise	....
SE	45°	clockwise	....
NE	90°	anticlockwise	....
SW	45°	anticlockwise	....
S	180°	clockwise	....

5

These are the nets of solids. What solids will they make? Choose four from: square-based pyramid, triangular-based pyramid, triangular prism, pentagonal prism, cube, cuboid, sphere or cone.

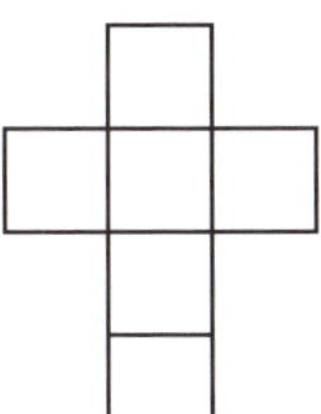

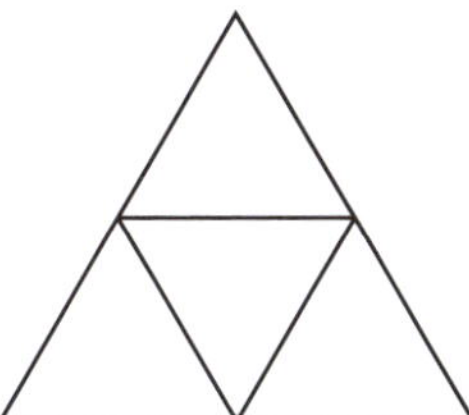

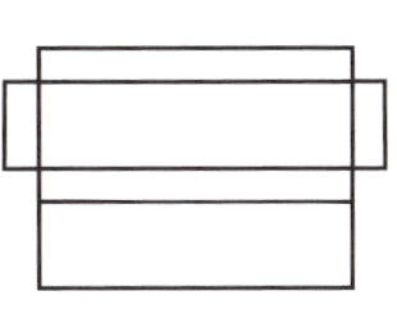

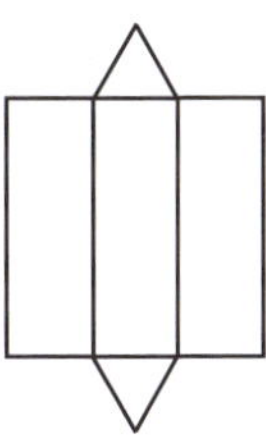

37 .... **38** .... **39** **40** 4

Look at these shapes.

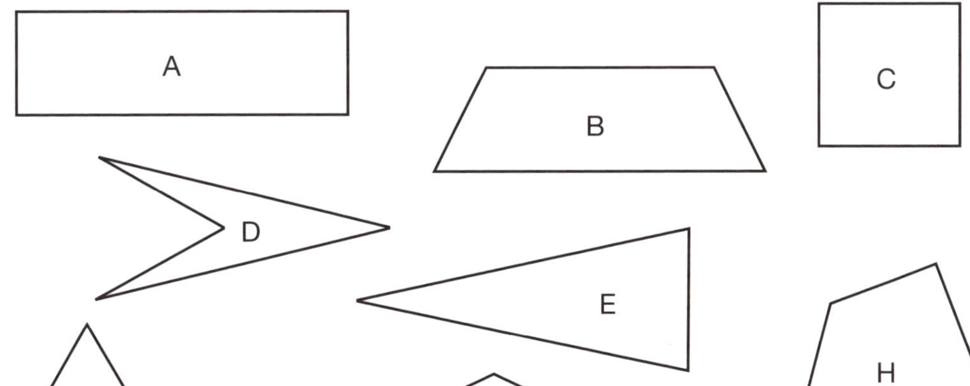

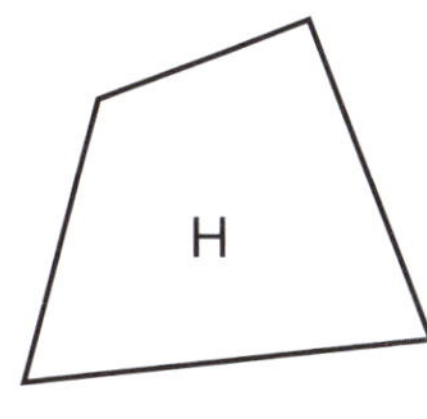

F

G

41 Which shape has no line of symmetry? 1

42 Which shapes have one line of symmetry? ...., ..., and

.... 3

43 Which shape has two lines of symmetry? 1

44 Which shape has more than three lines of symmetry? 1

Test Paper 2

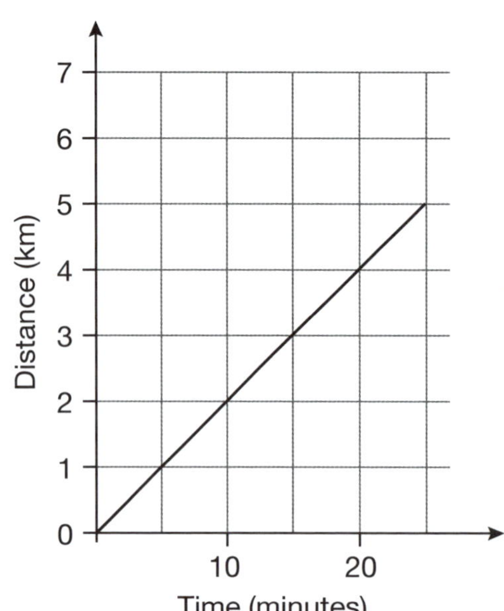

Look at the line graph and then answer these questions.

45 I'll do 2 km in .... minutes. 1

46 I'll do 1 km in .... minutes. 1

47 How far will I travel in 25 minutes? 1

48 What is my speed in km/h? 1

Here are the number of music CDs these 6 friends had.

Name	Pete	Lucy	Kath	Jez	Helen	Simone
Number	8	5	14	19	14	12

49 What is the mode? 1

50 What is the median? 1

51 What is the range? 1

52 What is the mean? 1

Here is a pie chart which shows how many computers pupils in Class 6C have at home.

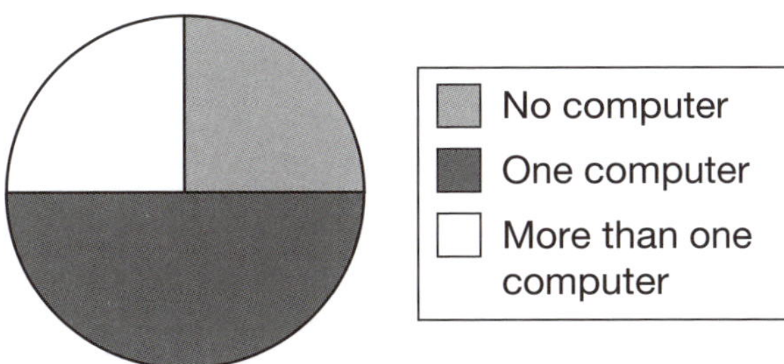

53 What percentage of pupils have at least one computer at home? 1

54 What fraction of pupils have more than one computer at home? 1

If there are 32 pupils in Class 6C:

55 How many do not have a computer at home? 1

56 How many have at least one computer at home? 1

Consider a fair dice 1 to 6.

What is the probability of rolling:

57 a 4 or a 5? 1

58 a whole number greater than 0 and less than 7? 1

59 The perimeter of a square is 28 cm. What is its area? 1

60 There are 630 children in a school. There are 5 boys to every 4 girls.

There are .... boys and .... girls. 2

Total 80

Test Paper 2

Keywords

Some special maths words are used in this book. You will find them **in bold** the first time they appear in the book. These words are explained here.

acute angle an angle that is less than a right angle

area how much space there is inside a 2D shape, measured in square units, for example, cm^2, m^2, km^2

capacity the maximum amount that a container can hold

composite a number that has more than 2 factors, so it can be divided by 1, the number itself and at least 1 other number

coordinates these indicate the position of a point on a graph, for example, (3,4). The first number is the distance you move in the x-direction; the second number is the distance you move in the y-direction.

cube number a number that is made by multiplying the number by itself 3 times

edge the line where two faces join

equivalent equal in value or amount

face a flat side of a solid object

factor the factors of a number are numbers that divide into it with no remainder. For example 1, 2, 4 and 8 are all factors of 8

improper fraction a fraction with the numerator bigger than the denominator

lowest term the simplest you can make a fraction, for example $\frac{4}{10}$ reduced to the lowest term is $\frac{2}{5}$.

mixed number a number that contains a whole number and a fraction, for example, $5\frac{1}{2}$ is a mixed number

multiples just extended times tables. They are the original number multiplied by another number

negative number a number that is less than zero and is shown with a minus symbol in front of the number

obtuse angle an angle that is more than 90° and not more than 180°

parallel always the same distance apart

perimeter	the total distance around the edge of a 2D shape
polygon	a closed shape with three or more sides
power	the number of times a number is multiplied by itself, for example $3^4 = 3 \times 3 \times 3 \times 3$
prime number	a whole number greater than 1 that has only 2 factors: 1 and the number itself
product	a number or a quantity that you get by multiplying two or more numbers or expressions together
reflex angle	an angle that is bigger than 180° and less than 360° 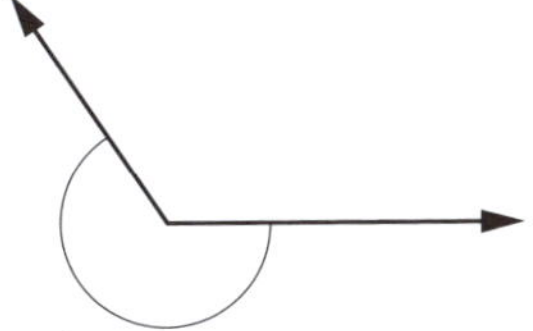
square number	a number that is made by multiplying the number by itself
vertex, vertices	the point where two or more edges or sides in a shape meet
volume	the amount of space a solid 3D object takes up, measured in cm^3 or m^3.

11+ Study Guide

Essentials

- Don't worry too much about the level that you start at. Beginning with an easier book can help your confidence.
- Make sure you have the right equipment – you will need your pencils, an eraser, and a notebook.
- This book contains skills guidance and worked examples, but if you need more help with technique, the Bond Handbooks might also be useful to you.

Studying Effectively

1. Turn to the first topic and read the Key Skills box. You might want to read it a few times or with someone else to understand it properly or to underline key words.
2. Read the worked example a few times and make sure you understand it.
3. In your notebook, write down the topic heading and the worked example on a new page. This is for you to revise and remember. Once you have completed the final book, you will have a super-useful notebook that you can use in secondary school.
4. Now set a timer – a kitchen timer, a watch or phone with an alarm – for the timed section.
5. Work your way through the questions carefully. If you don't know the answer to something, draw a circle around the question number and take your best guess. This is important as you can find patterns if you make mistakes and it highlights where you need to consolidate.
6. Ask someone to mark the paper for you or mark it yourself and see where you made mistakes. Is there a common pattern? For every mistake, decide if it is not knowing the technique properly, not consolidating the technique enough or a loss of focus and label this next to each question using T = technique, C = consolidation, F = focus.
7. Have another go at the questions you made errors in to understand what you did wrong. If it is vocabulary problem, write down the word with its meaning / synonym / antonym at the back of your book so that you widen your vocabulary range.

Making Mistakes

Everyone makes mistakes and they are an important part of how we learn. The reason we practise before an exam is so that we can make those mistakes in a safe space rather than in the test itself and that way we can learn from them and make fewer mistakes when it really matters.

Remember that there is no such thing as a 'silly mistake'. You are not silly, and neither is your mistake. It is usually not understanding the technique, not consolidating the skill needed so that it is only partially remembered, or you have lost focus. Losing focus does not mean that you have done something bad, it just means that your attention was on something else. These tips can help:

Not Understanding the Technique:

- Go back to the learning section and reread the key skills box.
- Look at the worked example that you have in your notebook.
- Use the Bond Handbook for more support.

Not Consolidating Enough:

- It is amazing how much consolidation is needed by everyone so don't worry about doing lots of additional questions.
- Look at Bond online for some more questions to help you revise.
- Ask someone to test you on the technique.

Losing Focus:

- Make sure that you are not too tired, hungry, thirsty or distracted.
- Work out where you have made a mistake and break it down into sections. It might be that you focus on tricky division, but go too fast when it comes to addition. It might be that you read the comprehension extract, but you lost focus and misread it.
- Once you have identified the problem area, make sure that in new questions, you check yourself and focus carefully.

Common Problems

'I don't have time to study.'

Make sure that you have a timetable that is doable. If you have lots of activities that take up time, perhaps break your work up. The books all have timing sections so fit in smaller sections when you can. It's important to talk to your parent if you feel that you need more time for your 11+ work.

'I find it hard to complete my homework as I want to play instead.'

Motivation is difficult for most people. Don't completely stop all fun activities during the 11+ but get a balance. Key to this is a timetable so you know when, what and where to study. Make sure it is doable and build in something fun if you complete your homework for the day. Another tip is to write down your reasons for doing the 11+. It might be to keep your family happy, to get into a school your friends are going to, or even that the school is convenient. Ask yourself how important each reason is. Can you commit to the reasons you have? If so, keep remembering the reason and what will happen if you don't commit? Perhaps talk to your family so that they know how you feel.

'My friend is using different books to me.'

The Bond 11+ system covers English/Verbal Reasoning and Maths/Non-verbal reasoning/spatial awareness. Bond has had many decades of success in 11+ material. Many tutors will only use Bond for their pupils, and they get an exceptionally high pass rate. It doesn't mean that Bond is the only 11+ provider, so don't worry that your friend is using different material. What is important is that you are fully prepared for your CEM online exam, and you can have confidence in the Bond system.

'I'm scared of failing.'

It is natural to feel that. Remember that you cannot climb a mountain in one gigantic step. You need lots and lots of little steps to get to the top. The 11+ is like that. You can't sit down and learn everything straight away, but the little steps you take will lead you to the exam. Remember that every mistake can be identified and once you identify it, you may be able to understand it and solve the problem for next time. Mistakes are perfection in progress! If a selective school is the best learning environment for you, then you can work little and often through the books and then test papers leading up to the exam. If you find it too much and you are working at your full potential already, then maybe a school that is not selective will suit your learning better. There is no 'best school' and 'worst school' for everyone. It is the best school for an individual child. Do talk to someone about your feelings though as you need to feel supported.

'My friend has a tutor. Do I need one?'

Whether or not to have tutor depends on many different factors, including where your particular strengths and challenges lie, your own approach to learning, and whether your parents are comfortable with the costs involved. The Bond system is rigorous and aims to support every child with a range of books and learning materials. The Bond Handbooks can do the job of a tutor and many tutors also use the Bond books and Handbooks with their pupils. Bond has been providing 11+ material since the 1960s, helping thousands of pupils to pass their 11+ exams without having a tutor.

'I don't want to do the 11+ exam.'

This is a conversation to have with your family, but the best advice might be to follow the 11+ books anyway. They will teach you skills, techniques and methods that will give you self-confidence regardless of the secondary school you attend. No knowledge is a waste, and you will be keeping your options open. There is more information on the Bond website. Bond has a Parent's Guide to the 11+ and there is a range of supportive printed and online material. See online for further details. **www.bond11plus.co.uk**

Progress Chart

Learning Papers

Basic Number Skills

/30

Decimals, Fractions and Percentages

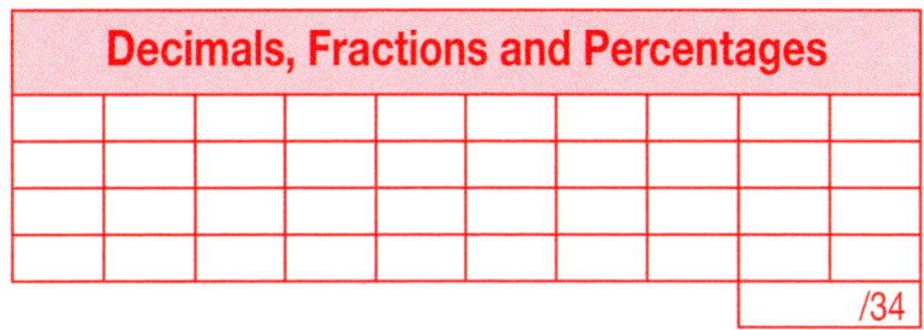

/34

Proportion and Ratio

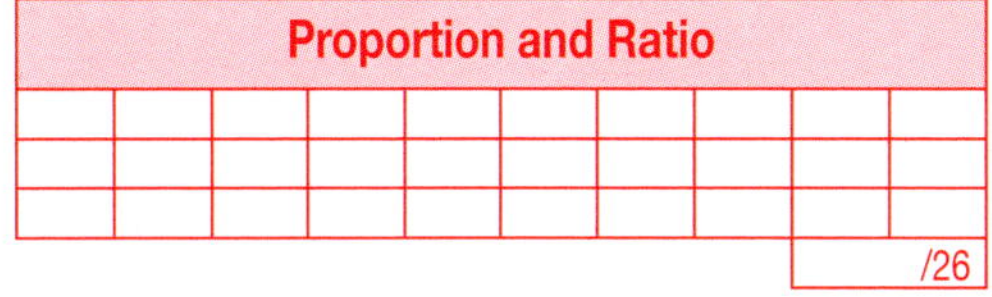

/26

BIDMAS, Sequences and Algebra

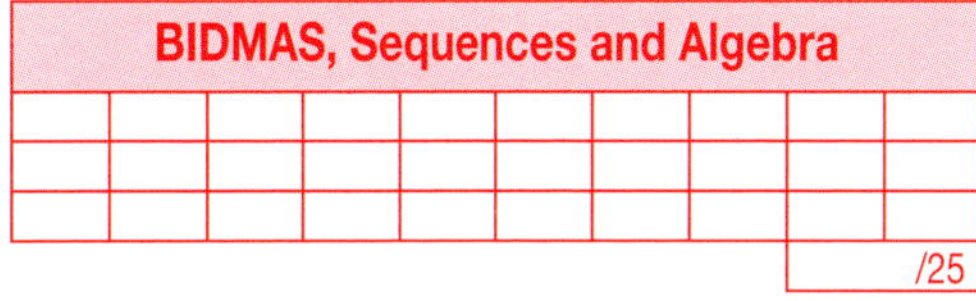

/25

Measures

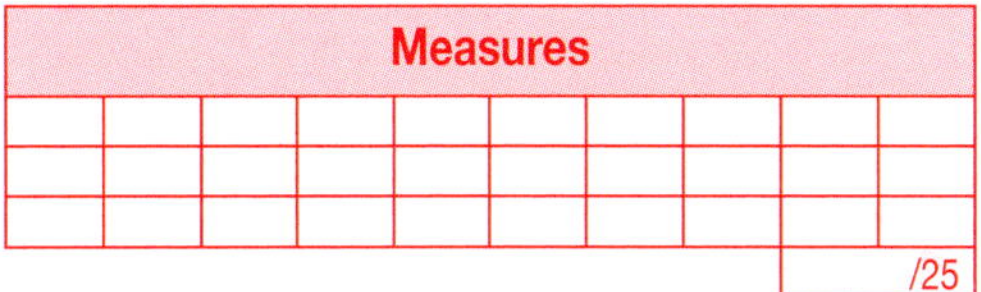

/25

Shape, Space, Position and Direction

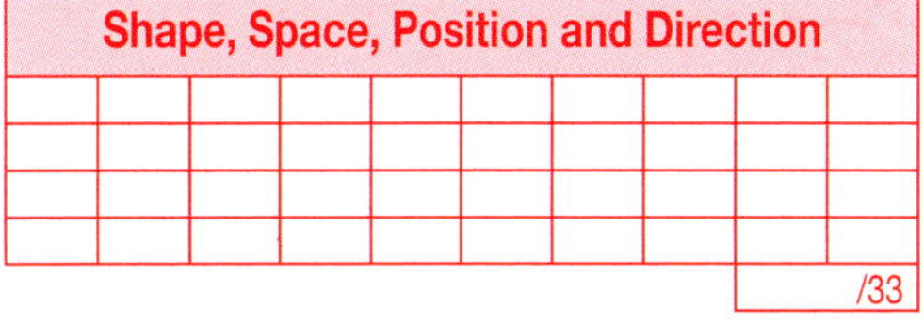

/33

Statistics and Probability

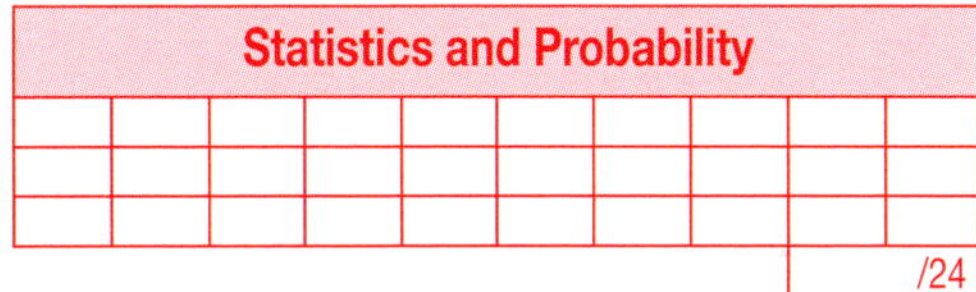

/24

Word and Logic Problems

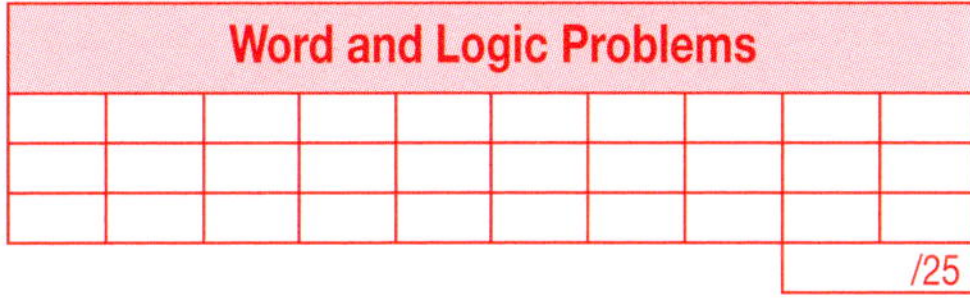

/25

Curveball Questions 1

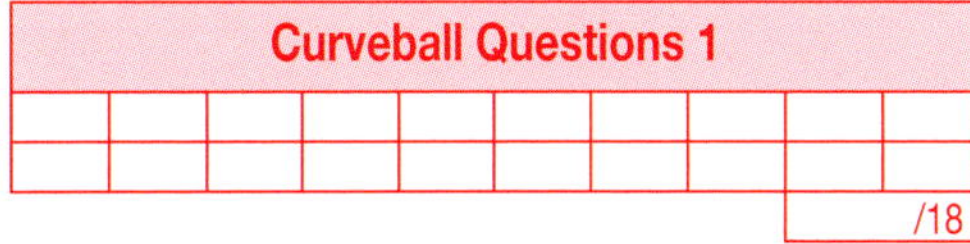

/18

Curveball Questions 2

/10

Test Papers

Test Paper 1

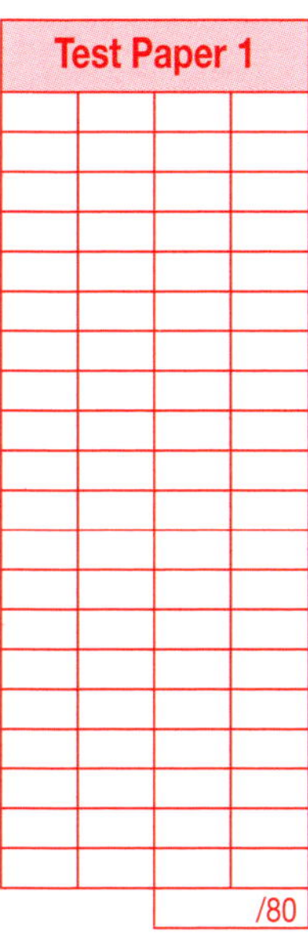

/80

Test Paper 2

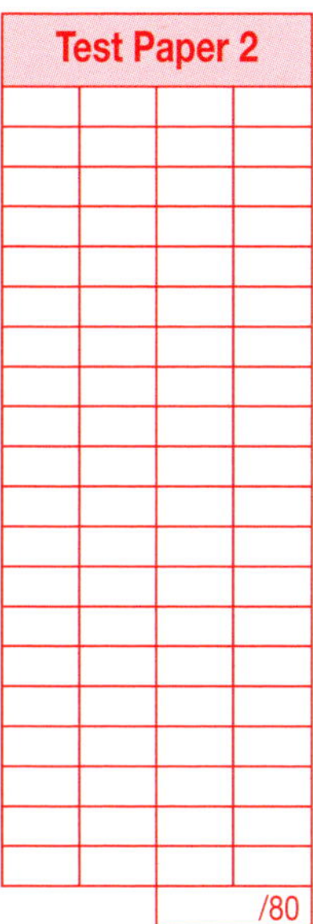

/80

Mixed Papers

	1	2	3	4
1				
2				
3				
4				
5				
6				
7				
8				
9				
10				
11				
12				
13				
14				
15				
16				
17				
18				
19				
20				
21				
22				
23				
24				
25				
26				
27				
28				
29				
30				
31				
32				
33				
34				
35				
36				
37				
38				
39				
40				
	/40	/40	/40	/40

Bond 11+

Ages 10–11+

Maths

Assessment Practice

Book 1

ANSWERS

AND PROGRESS CHART

OXFORD

Answers

Learning Paper: Basic Number Skills

1 **1.7** 10 tenths is 1 and 7 tenths is 0.7.
2 **1.43** 100 hundredths is 1, 40 hundredths is 0.4 and 3 hundredths is 0.03.
3 **47** 40 ones is 40 and 7 ones is 7.
4–7 When rounding a number to the nearest whole number, look at the number in the tenths column. If it is 4 or below, leave the number in the ones column unchanged. If it is 5 or above, raise the number in the ones column by 1.
4 **8** The 0.3 in 8.35 rounds down to 8.
5 **1** The 0.7 in 0.71 rounds up to 1.
6 **4** The 0.4 in 4.48 rounds down to 4.
7 **0** The 0.1 in 0.123 rounds down to 0.
8 **6.837** Adjust the numbers so that they have an equal amount of digits: 3.7 is the same as 3.700; 2.95 is the same as 2.950.

	3	·	7	0	0
	2	·	9	5	0
+	0	·	1	8	7
	6	**·**	**8**	**3**	**7**
	1		1		

9 **1.511** Adjust the numbers so that they have an equal amount of digits: 3.2 is the same as 3.200.

	^{2}3	·	^{11}2	^{9}0	^{1}0
–	1	·	6	8	9
	1	**·**	**5**	**1**	**1**

10 **47** 799 ÷ 17 = 47

		0	**4**	**7**
1	7	7	^{7}9	^{11}9

11 **Montreal** With a temperature of –10°C, Montreal was coldest.
12 **30°C** 27°C – –3°C = 27°C + 3°C = 30°C
13 **31°C** 26°C – –5°C = 26°C + 5°C = 31°C
14 **41°C** 31°C – –10°C = 31°C + 10°C = 41°C
15 **18, 27, 36** Keep adding the same number. (9)
16 **24, 36, 48** Keep adding the same number. (12)
17 **43** All the others will divide by 3.
18 **1, 3, 7, 21** The factors of a number are the numbers that divide exactly into it (1 × 21 = 21; 3 × 7 = 21).
19 **2, 3, 5** To find the prime factors of a number, divide by prime numbers. Try each prime number in turn, starting with the smallest, until the result is also prime. 60 ÷ 2 = 30; 30 ÷ 2 = 15; 15 ÷ 3 = 5. The prime factors of 60 are 2 and 3 and 5.
20–22 Composite numbers must have more than 2 factors, so they are not 1 or the prime numbers. The prime numbers from 1 to 100 are: 2, 3, 5, 7, 11, 13, 17, 19, 23, 29, 31, 37, 41, 43, 47, 53, 59, 61, 67, 71, 73, 79, 83, 89, 97.
20 **23**
21 **59**
22 **48**
23 **10^4**
24 **7^3**
25 **1^6**

Learning Paper: Decimals, Fractions and Percentages

1–4 To divide by 10, place the numbers in a decimal grid using hundreds, tens, ones, tenths, hundredths, thousandths, etc. Divide a number by 10 by moving it one place to the right.
1 **7.865**

T	O	·	t	h	th
7	8	·	6	5	
	7	·	8	6	5

2 **0.654**

T	O	·	t	h	th
	6	·	5	4	
	0	·	6	5	4

3 **46.75**

H	T	O	·	t	h
4	6	7	·	5	
	4	6	·	7	5

4 **0.0123**

O	·	t	h	th	tth
0	·	1	2	3	
0	·	0	1	2	3

5–8 To divide by 1000, place the numbers in a decimal grid using hundreds, tens, ones, tenths, hundredths, thousandths, etc. Divide a number by 1000 by moving the digits three places to the right.
5 **0.385**

O	T	O	·	t	h	th
3	8	5				
		0	·	3	8	5

6 **0.00012**

O	·	t	h	th	tth	hth
0	·	1	2			
0	·	0	0	0	1	2

7 **0.0078**

H	·	t	h	th	hth
7	·	8			
0	·	0	0	7	8

8 **0.049**

T	O	·	t	h	th
4	9				
	0	·	0	4	9

9 **100** 4.9 × 100 = 490
10 **1.23** 1.23 ÷ 10 = 0.123
11 **13.6** 0.136 × 100 = 13.6

12–13 There are five increments between 6.3 and 6.4. Take the difference between these numbers (6.4 – 6.3 = 0.1) and divide it by the number of increments (0.1 ÷ 5 = 0.02). Then label each increment (e.g. 6.32, 6.34, 6.36, 6.38).

12 **6.34**

13 **6.42**

14 **7.88, 7.8, 7.088, 7.008** To order the decimals, look at the ones first, then the tenths, then the hundredths and then the thousandths. Remember that 7.8 is the same as 7.80 or 7.800.

15–20 To find equivalent fractions, multiply the numerator and the denominator by the same number.

15 **20** 5 × 5 = 25; 4 × 5 = 20

16 **77** 11 × 11 = 121; 7 × 11 = 77

17 **56** 8 × 8 = 64; 7 × 8 = 56

18 **12** 7 × 6 = 42; 2 × 6 = 12

19 **36** 4 × 12 = 48; 3 × 12 = 36

20 **49** 9 × 7 = 63; 7 × 7 = 49

21 $\mathbf{\frac{3}{8}, \frac{1}{2}, \frac{2}{3}, \frac{3}{4}, \frac{5}{6}}$ First find equivalent fractions so that the bottom numbers (the denominators) are all the same. $\frac{1}{2} = \frac{12}{24}$; $\frac{2}{3} = \frac{16}{24}$; $\frac{5}{6} = \frac{20}{24}$; $\frac{3}{8} = \frac{9}{24}$; $\frac{3}{4} = \frac{18}{24}$ Then compare the top numbers (numerators). $\frac{9}{24} < \frac{12}{24} < \frac{16}{24} < \frac{18}{24} < \frac{20}{24}$ therefore the order is: $\frac{3}{8}, \frac{1}{2}, \frac{2}{3}, \frac{3}{4}, \frac{5}{6}$

22 **70, 490** Divide 560 by 8 to find the number of pupils absent (560 ÷ 8 = 70); take this number away from 560 to find the number of pupils present (560 – 70 = 490).

23–24 To add fractions together, first find equivalent fractions so that the bottom numbers (the denominators) are the same. Remember to only add the top numbers (the numerators), not the denominators. Then put the answer in its simplest form by dividing the numerator and denominator by the same number, making both numbers as small as possible.

23 $\mathbf{1\frac{1}{16}}$ $\frac{5}{8} = \frac{10}{16}$; $\frac{10}{16} + \frac{7}{16} = \frac{17}{16} = 1\frac{1}{16}$

24 $\mathbf{2\frac{7}{9}}$ $7 = \frac{63}{9}$; $4\frac{2}{9} = \frac{38}{9}$; $\frac{63}{9} - \frac{38}{9} = \frac{25}{9} = 2\frac{7}{9}$

25 **18, 12** To find 60%, work out 10% (by dividing by 10) and multiply the result by 6 (30 ÷ 10 = 3; 3 × 6 = 18). This is the number of girls. Subtract the number of girls from the total number of children to find the number of boys (30 – 18 = 12).

Learning Paper: Proportion and Ratio

1 **£5.36** Divide the total cost by 11 to find the cost of a single item (£7.37 ÷ 11 = £0.67). Then multiply this number by 8 (£0.67 × 8 = £5.36).

2 **£7.70** Divide the total cost by 9 to find the cost of a single item (£6.30 ÷ 9 = £0.70). Then multiply this number by 11 (£0.70 × 11 = £7.70).

3–5 Find the equivalent cost for 1 kg at each size. There are 1000 grams in a kilogram. A: 1 kg costs £3.81; B 1000 g ÷ 200 g = 5, so 1 kg costs 5 × £1.10 = £5.50; C 1000 g ÷ 125 g = 8, so 1 kg costs 8 × £0.54 = £4.32; D 1000 g ÷ 250 g = 4, so 1 kg costs 4 × £0.93 = £3.72; E 1000 g ÷ 750 g = $\frac{4}{3}$ so 1 kg costs $\frac{4}{3}$ × £3.97= £5.29; F 1000 g ÷ 400 g = 2.5, so 1 kg costs 2.5 × £1.56 = £3.90.

3 **D** With a cost of £3.72 per kilogram, Tin D was the best bargain.

4 **A** With a cost of £3.81 per kilogram, Tin A was the second best bargain.

5 **F** With a cost of £3.90 per kilogram, Tin F was the third best bargain.

6 **£0.84 or 84p** Divide the total cost by 13 to find the cost of a single item (£1.56 ÷ 13 = £0.12). Then multiply this number by 7 (£0.12 × 7 = £0.84 or 84p).

7 **5 kg** £6.00 ÷ £1.20 = 5

8 **0.25 kg or 250 g** £1.20 ÷ £0.30 = 4; 1 kg ÷ 4 = 0.25 kg or 250 g

9 **£4.20** £1.20 × 3.5 kg = £4.20

10 **189** 7 + 6 = 13; 351 ÷ 13 = 27; 7 × 27 = 189

11 **162** 6 × 27 = 162

12 **84, 42, 21** Work backwards through the calculation. For every 1p coin, there are two 2p coins and therefore four 5p coins. Therefore the amounts in the ratio of 1p coins : 2p coins : 5p coins is 1p : 4p : 20p. Add these amounts to find 25p then divide £5.25 by 25p (525 ÷ 25 = 21); multiply the amounts in the ratio by 21 to find 21p : 84p : 420p. Then divide by each coin to find the number (21 ÷ 1p = 21; 84 ÷ 2p = 42; and 420p ÷ 5 = 84). Then reverse the numbers, so the ratio is shown in the same order: 5p : 2p; 1p = 84 : 42 : 21

13 **60, 30, 15** If Tom was 1 year old, Uncle John would be 2 years old and Grandma would be 4 years old. This gives the ratio 1:2:4. To solve a ratio, add up the ratio numbers (1 + 2 + 4 = 7). Then divide this number into the total of their ages (105 ÷ 7 = 15). Finally, multiply this number by the individual ratios to find the ages (Tom is 1 × 15 = 15 years old, Uncle John is 2 × 15 = 30 years old and Grandma is 4 × 15 = 60 years old).

14–16 To solve a ratio, add up the ratio numbers (1 + 3 + 5 = 9). Then divide this number into the number of pencils (36 ÷ 9 = 4). Finally, multiply this number by the individual parts.

14 **4** 4 × 1

15 **12** 4 × 3

16 **20** 4 × 5

17 **£4.00, £3.50, £2.50** To solve a ratio, add up the ratio numbers (8 + 7 + 5 = 20). Then divide this number into the total sum of money (£10.00 ÷ 20 = 50p). Finally, multiply this answer by the individual ratios (Emma gets 8 × 50p = £4.00; Salim gets 7 × 50p = £3.50; Katie gets 5 × 50p = £2.50).

18 **27, 9, 3** For every 1 sweet that Prue has, Ragini has 3 and Penny has 9. This gives the ratio 1:3:9. To solve a ratio, add up the ratio numbers (1 + 3 + 9 = 13). Then divide this number into the number of sweets (39 ÷ 13 = 3). Finally, multiply this number by the individual ratios (Prue has 1 × 3 = 3; Ragini has 3 × 3 = 9; Penny has 9 × 3 = 27).

Learning Paper: BIDMAS, Sequences and Algebra

1–4 The pattern here is that each triangle has the same number of dots as the number of the triangle squared, so the first triangle has 1 dot ($1^2 = 1$), the second triangle has 4 dots ($2^2 = 4$) and so on. When a new row is added to form the triangle shape, the total number of dots gives a squared number: the first triangle has 1 dot ($1^2 = 1$), the second triangle has 4 dots ($2^2 = 4$) and so on.

1 **25** The fifth triangle will have 25 dots because $5^2 = 25$.

2 **49** The seventh triangle will have 49 dots because $7^2 = 49$.

3 **121** The eleventh triangle will have 121 dots because $11^2 = 121$.

4 **400** The twentieth triangle will have 400 dots because $20^2 = 400$.

5 **27** 1000 ÷ 38 = 26.32; round up to the next complete page.

6–9 This is BIDMAS. Complete the equation in the brackets first, then the multiplication or division, then the addition or subtraction.

6 **5** (7 × 8) + 5 = 61; 7 × 8 = 56 then 61 – 56 = 5

7 **2** (9 × 12) – 2 = 106; 9 × 12 = 108 then 108 – 106 = 2

8 **3** 8 × (7 – 3) = 32; 8 × 4 = 32 then 7 – 4 = 3

9 **5** 6 × (11 – 5) = 36; 6 × 6 = 36 then 11 – 6 = 5

10–13 When filling in a missing symbol, check the answer by reversing the equation. The reversals are shown in brackets below.

10 **+** (52 – 7 = 45)

11 **÷** (33 ÷ 11 = 3)

12 **x** (37 968 ÷ 678 = 56)

13 **÷** (18 × 5 = 90)

14–17 When filling in a missing symbol, check the answer by reversing the equation. The reversals are shown in brackets below.

14 **÷** (5 × 14.8 = 74)

15 **+** (79 – 5 = 74)

16 **–** (69 + 5 = 74)

17 **×** (370 ÷ 5 = 74)

18–21 To solve this type of question, work out the calculation on the right-hand side of the equation. This will be equal to the calculation on the left-hand side of the equation.

18 **10** 2 × 10 = 4 × 5; 4 × 5 = 20 and 2 × 10 = 20

19 **5** 5 × 5 = 27 – 2; 27 – 2 = 25 and 5 × 5 = 25

20 **4** 12 × 3 = 36 ÷ 3; 36 ÷ 3 = 12 and 4 × 3 = 12

21 **5** 5 × 4 = 10 + 10; 10 + 10 = 20 and 5 × 4 = 20

22 **3** Complete the subtraction first (10 – 1 = 9). That gives $3y = 9$, so $9 \div 3 = y$. 9 ÷ 3 = 3, so $y = 3$.

23 **4** Complete the subtraction first ($4y - y = 3y$). That gives $3y = 12$, so $12 \div 3 = y$. 12 ÷ 3 = 4, so $y = 4$.

24 **2** Complete the addition first ($2y + y = 3y$). That gives $3y = 6$, so $6 \div 3 = y$. 6 ÷ 3 = 2, so $y = 2$.

25 **3** Complete the addition first ($3y + y = 4y$ and 11 + 1 = 12). That gives $4y = 12$, so $12 \div 4 = y$. 12 ÷ 4 = 3, so $y = 3$.

Learning Paper: Measures

1–4 To find the area of a triangle, multiply the height by the length and then divide by 2.

1 **6 cm²** 4 squares long × 3 squares high = 12 cm²; 12 cm² ÷ 2 = 6 cm²

2 **12 cm²** 6 squares long × 4 squares high = 24 cm²; 24 cm² ÷ 2 = 12 cm²

3 **10 cm²** 4 squares long × 5 squares high = 20 cm²; 20 cm² ÷ 2 = 10 cm²

4 **12 cm²** 6 squares long × 4 squares high = 24 cm²; 24 cm² ÷ 2 = 12 cm²

5–7 To find the area, multiply the base by the height.

5 **60 cm²** 10 cm × 6 cm = 60 cm²

6 **30 cm²** 5 cm × 6 cm = 30 cm²

7 **50 cm²** 5 cm × 10 cm = 50 cm²

8–10 To find the perimeter, add the length of each of the sides together.

8 **32 cm** 10 cm + 6 cm + 10 cm + 6 cm = 32 cm

9 **22 cm** 5 cm + 6 cm + 5 cm + 6 cm = 22 cm

10 **30 cm** 10 cm + 5 cm + 10 cm + 5 cm = 30 cm

11 **480 cm³** 12 cm × 5 cm × 8 cm = 480 cm³; All the measurements are in cm, so just multiply together.

12 **480 000 mm³** 120 mm × 50 mm × 80 mm = 480 000 mm³; Convert all the measurements to mm, then multiply together.

13 **0.96 m³** 1 m × 0.8 m × 1.2 m = 0.96 m³; Convert all the measurements in m, then multiply together. There are 100 centimetres in a metre, so to convert centimetres to metres, divide by 100. When multiplying decimals, you can just ignore the decimal points to begin with, multiply 8 × 12 = 96 and then say 'There were two decimal places, so I have to put those back in my answer now': 0.8 × 1.2 = 0.96

14 **2.45** 245 cm ÷ 100 = 2.45 m

15 **13.42** 1342 cm ÷ 100 = 13.42 m

16 **123.45** 12 345 cm ÷ 100 = 123.45 m

17 **97 kg** There are 1000 kg in 1 tonne; so 0.225 tonnes × 1000 = 225 kg; 225 kg – 128 kg = 97 kg

18 **625** There are 1000 grams in a kilogram; 1000 g – 375 g = 625 g.

19 **0.45** 450 cm³ ÷ 1000 = 0.45 litres.

20 **108** 27 litres × 4 = 108 litres.

21 **1.8** 600 cm³ × 3 = 1800 cm³ = 1800 cm³ ÷ 1000 = 1.8 litres.

22–25 To use a world time chart, begin with the first country and add or subtract the number of hours to find the time in another country.

22 **03:00** Japan is +9 hours from London, so to find the time in London when it is midday in Japan, subtract 9 hours (12:00–9 hours = 03:00).

23 **11:00** Japan is +1 hour from Hong Kong (Hong Kong is +8 from London and Japan is +9, so there is a 1-hour difference). To find the time in Hong Kong when it is midday in Japan, subtract 1 hour (12:00 – 1 hour = 11:00).

24 **11:00** Cyprus is +2 hours from London and Austria is +1 hour, so there is a 1-hour difference. If it is midday in Cyprus, subtract 1 hour to find the time in Austria (12:00 – 1 hour = 11:00).

25 **8:36 a.m.** Hong Kong is +8 hours from London, so if it is 4:36 p.m. in Hong Kong, then subtract 8 hours to find the time in London (4:36 p.m. – 8 hours = 8:36 a.m.).

Learning Paper: Shape, Space, Position and Direction

1–3 Each quarter is 90° and contains 3 numbers, so each number is equal to 30° (90° ÷ 3 = 30°).

1 **60°** 2 × 30° = 60°

2 **150°** 5 × 30° = 150°

3 **120°** 4 × 30° = 120°

4–6 Angles on a straight line add up to 180°.

4 **85°** 180° = 50° + p° + 45°; 180° – 50° – 45° = 85°

5 **60°** 180° = q° + q° + q°; 180° = 3q°, so q° = 180° ÷ 3 = 60°

6 **66.5°** 180° = r° + 47° + r°; 180° = 2r° + 47°, so 2r° = 133° and r° = 133 ÷ 2 = 66.5°

7–10 An acute angle is less than 90°. A right angle is exactly 90°. An obtuse angle is greater than 90° but less than 180°. A reflex angle is greater than 180°.

7 **obtuse angle**

8 **right angle**

9 **acute angle**

10 **reflex angle**

11 When plotting coordinates on a grid, use the rule "along the corridor and up the stairs" to remember to go horizontal, then vertical.

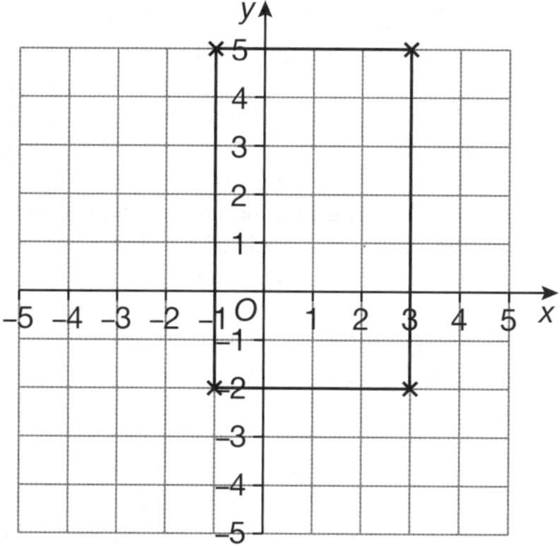

12 **(–1, –2)**

13 The shape has 1 set of parallel lines; 1 shorter and 1 longer.

14 **rhombus** The shape has 2 sets of parallel sides; all 4 sides the same length; 1 pair are diagonal.

15 **parallelogram** The shape has 2 sets of parallel sides; 2 longer and 2 shorter sides, 1 pair are diagonal.

16 **rectangle** The shape has 2 sets of parallel sides; 2 longer and 2 shorter sides, 1 pair are diagonal.

17 **kite** The shape has 2 shorter and 2 longer sides.

18 A face is a flat surface of a 3D shape, an edge is a straight line where two faces meet and a vertex is a corner where three or more faces meet.

Name of solid	Faces	Vertices	Edges
Triangular prism	5	6	9
Square prism	6	8	12

19 **none** Cube A has 2 light grey sides so it cannot be a match. Both Cube B and C have one face that is black, so they cannot be correct either.

20 **A** Cube A has 2 light grey sides and 1 dark grey side.

21 **B** Cube A has 2 light grey sides so it cannot be a match. Cube C has 1 side with a grid pattern, so it cannot be a match either.

22 **none** Cube A has 2 light grey sides so it cannot be a match. Cube B has 1 side with a wave pattern so it cannot be a match. In the net the light grey side and the black side are in opposite positions, so they cannot be adjacent as they are in cube C.

23 **C** Cube A has 2 light grey sides so it cannot be a match. Cube B has a 1 side with a wave pattern so it cannot be a match.

24

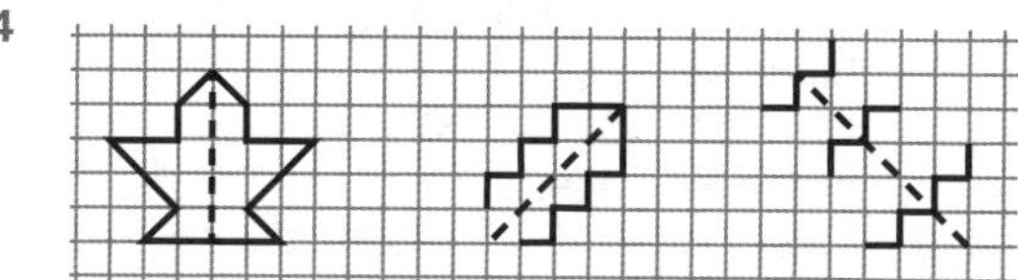

Learning Paper: Statistics and Probability

1

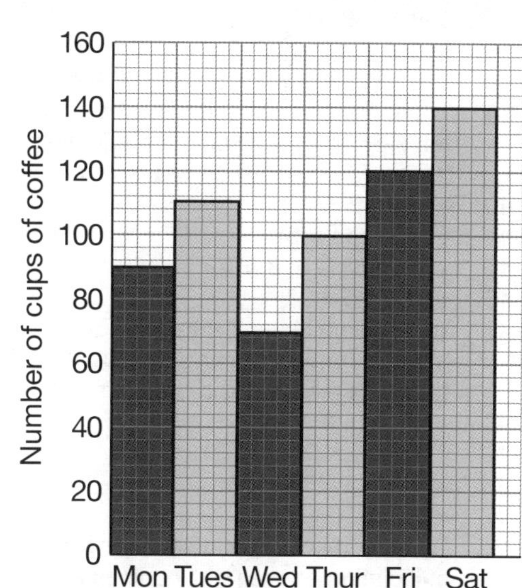

2–4 To use the conversion graph, remember that the miles are read on the vertical line (y axis) and the kilometres are read on the bottom horizontal line (x axis).

2 **Darlington 40 km; Newcastle 80 km** Look at the vertical axis and find 25 miles (midway between 20 and 30). Follow the line across to the right until reaching the diagonal line. Then read down to find that 25 miles is the same as 40 kilometres. To convert the other figure, follow the same process. Another way of working it out would be to use doubling: if 25 miles = 40 km then doubling both shows that 50 miles = 80 kilometres.

3 **60 miles** Find 95 km on the horizontal line. Follow it upwards until it touches the diagonal line, then read across to find 60 miles.

4 **50 miles** Find 75 km on the horizontal line. Follow it upwards until it touches the diagonal line, then read across. 75 km = 45 miles, so 50 miles is greater.

5 **26** The mode is the most common score. Two people scored 26.
6 **26** To find the median of a set of numbers, list them in order from smallest to largest (15, 26, 26, 31, 42). The median is the middle number.
7 **27** To find the range of a set of numbers, subtract the smallest value from the largest value (42 – 15 = 27).
8 **28** To find the mean of a set of numbers, add the numbers together and then divide the total by the quantity of numbers in the group (42 + 15 + 26 + 31 + 26 = 140; 140 ÷ 5 = 28).
9 **26** To find the median of a set of numbers, list them in order from smallest to largest (25, 26, 26, 31, 42). The median is the middle number.
10 **17** To find the range of a set of numbers, subtract the smallest value from the largest value (42 – 25 = 17).
11–13 To find the probability it is helpful to write out the 6 balls (1, 2, 3, 4, 5, 6) and then use those numbers to answer the questions.
11 $\mathbf{\frac{1}{2}}$ There are 3 even-numbered balls out of a total of 6, $\frac{3}{6} = \frac{1}{2}$.
12 $\mathbf{\frac{1}{6}}$ There is 1 ball numbered '5' out of a total of 6.
13 $\mathbf{\frac{1}{2}}$ There are 3 odd-numbered balls out of a total of 6, $\frac{3}{6} = \frac{1}{2}$.
14 **40, 50, 35** Add up all the numbers in each circle in the Venn diagram. 18 + 9 + 7 + 6 = 40 children like soul, 29 + 9 + 7 + 5 = 50 children like rock and 17 + 6 + 7 + 5 = 35 children like pop music.
15 **16** Add the numbers in the overlap between the circle for soul and the circle for rock (9 + 7 = 16).
16 **13** Add the numbers in the overlap between the circle for soul and the circle for pop (6 + 7 = 13).

Learning Paper: Word and Logic Problems

1 **8** 1500p ÷ 175p = 8.571; round down to the nearest whole number to find the number of comics.
2 **124** There are 1000 grams in a kilogram; 3000 ÷ 125 g = 24 packets.
3 **£2.49** Subtract the change from £20 to find how much Jenny spent (£20 – £2.57 = £17.43). Divide by 7 to find the price per metre (£17.43 ÷ 7 = £2.49 per metre).
4 **£4.20** Subtract the cost of the toy from the selling price to find the profit on 1 toy (£1.60 – £1.25 = £0.35). Multiply by 12 to find the total profit on 12 toys (12 × £0.35 = £4.20).
5 **£1.05** £$\frac{1}{2}$ = 50p, £0.55 = 55p, 27p × 2 = 54p, £$\frac{13}{25}$ = £$\frac{52}{100}$ = 52p, £1.00 – 49p = 51p; 55p + 50p = £1.05
6 **125.75 m** 17.5 m × 7 = 122.5 m; 122.5 m + 3.25 m = 125.75 m
7 **£495** 12 × £37.50 = £450; £450 + £45 = £495
8 **6** 5000 ÷ 870 = 5.75; round the answer up to the nearest whole number of stands.
9 **988** Divide 1000 by 38 and round down the answer to the nearest whole number. Then multiply this number by 38.
10 **74** To find the number halfway between two numbers, add the 2 numbers together and then divide by 2 (37 + 111 = 148; 148 ÷ 2 = 74).
11 **8:00**
Bus A: 7:00, 7:05, 7:10, 7:15, 7:20, 7:25, 7:30, 7:35, 7:40, 7:45, 7:50, 7:55, 8:00
Bus B: 7:00, 7:15, 7:30, 7:45, 8:00
Bus C: 7:00, 7:12, 7:24, 7:36, 7:48, 8:00
12 **2040 m** Only count the space between each post; 24 × 85 = 2040 m
13 **2789** Subtract the number of men and children from the total population; 11 552 – 8763 = 2789
14 **5678** Subtract the number of men and women from the total population; 11 552 – 5874 = 5678
15 **3085** Subtract the number of women and the number of children from the total population; 11 552 – 2789 – 5678 = 3085
16 **45 m** 1.575 km = 1.575 × 1000 = 1575 m; 1575 m ÷ 35 = 45 m. Only count the space between each post.
17 **15** The average of the 4 numbers is $10\frac{1}{2}$, the total of the 4 numbers is 4 × $10\frac{1}{2}$ = 42. The average of 3 of the numbers is 9, so the total of these 3 numbers is 3 × 9 = 27. So the fourth number is 42 – 27 = 15.
18 **£0.80 or 80p** $\frac{3}{4}$ of the sum of money is £1.80. Divide by 3 to find $\frac{1}{4}$ (£1.80 ÷ 3 = £0.60), multiply by 4 to find the whole (£0.60 × 4 = £2.40) and finally divide by 3 to find $\frac{1}{3}$ (£2.40 ÷ 3 = £0.80 or 80p).
19 **23, 235, 218** Subtract the number of girls and teachers from the total to find the number of boys (476 – 241 = 235). Subtract the number of boys and teachers from the total to find the number of girls (476 – 258 = 218). Subtract the number of boys and the number of girls from the total to find the number of teachers (476 – 235 – 218 = 23).
20–21 An even number × an even number = an even number. An odd number × an odd number = an odd number. An even number × an odd number = an even number.
20 **EVEN**
21 **ODD**
22 **EVEN**
23 **EVEN**

Curveball Questions 1

1 **36** Find the factors of the numbers in the grid to help you place the numbers in the top row and first column. The total for the top row is: 12 + 2 + 1 + 3 + 10 + 8 = 36

×	12	2	1	3	10	8
6		12				
7						56
4		8		12		
9			9		90	
5	60					40
11						

2 **tetrahedron** The following diagram shows all the connections with the answer circled. The cylinder has 2 edges, the pentagonal prism has 15 edges, the hexagonal based pyramid has 12 edges, the tetrahedron has 6 edges and the square based pyramid 8 edges.

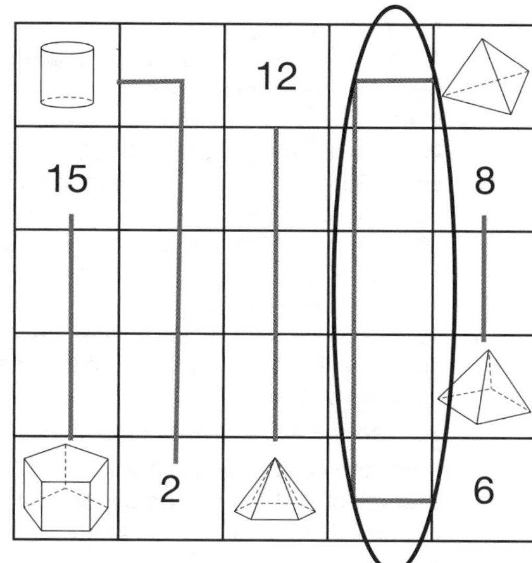

Mixed Paper 1

1 **102 021**

2 **4** $4^2 = 2 \times 2 = 4$

3 **25** $5^2 = 5 \times 5 = 25$

4 **9** $3^2 = 3 \times 3 = 9$

5 **36** $6^2 = 6 \times 6 = 36$

6 First, work out 20% of the prices provided. An easy way to do this is to work out 10% (by dividing by 10) and then doubling the result. This gives the VAT, which can be added to the 'Price Before VAT' to give the 'Total cost'.
£36.00, £216.00 10% of £180 is £18; £18 × 2 = £36; £180 + £36 = £216.00
£84.00, £504.00 10% of £420 is £42; £42 × 2 = £84; £420 + £84 = £504.00
£68.00, £408.00 10% of £340 is £34; £34 × 2 = £68; £340 + £68 = £408.00

Price before VAT	VAT	Total cost
£180.00	£36.00	£216.00
£420.00	£84.00	£504.00
£340.00	£68.00	£408.00

7 **0.7, 0.707, 0.708, 0.77, 0.78** To order the decimals, looks at the tenths first, then the hundredths and then the thousandths. Remember that 0.7 is the same as 0.70 or 0.700.

8 **185 boys; 222 girls** For every 11 children, if 6 are girls, then 5 are boys (11 – 6 = 5). Divide the total number of children in the school by 11 (407 ÷ 11 = 37). That means there are 37 groups of 11 children in the school, each with 5 boys and 6 girls. Multiply each number by 37 (5 × 37; 6 × 37) to find the total numbers of boys and girls

9 **24 cm²** Picture the shape as 2 rectangles. The top rectangle is 6 cm wide and 2 cm high. Multiply these two numbers to get the area (6 cm × 2 cm = 12 cm²). Now find the area of the bottom rectangle. The total height of the shape is 8 cm and the top rectangle is 2 cm, so the bottom rectangle must be 6 cm high (8 cm – 2 cm = 6 cm). The rectangle is 2 across, so multiplying the length and width gives 12 cm². Add the areas of the 2 rectangles to get the total area (12 cm² + 12 cm² = 24 cm²).

10 **28 cm** To find the perimeter, first add the missing measurements to the diagram. Working out question 19 showed that the sides of the bottom part of the 'T' are 6 cm each. The two sections on the underside of the crossbar must add up to 4 cm (6 cm – 2 cm = 4 cm). The next step is to add up all the measurements (6 cm + 2 cm + 2 cm + 6 cm + 2 cm + 6 cm + 2 cm + 2 cm = 28 cm).

11–13 There are 60 minutes in an hour, so a quarter of an hour is 15 minutes. Subtract this from the times given to get the correct answer.

11 **21:45**

12 **10:50**

13 **12:55**

14

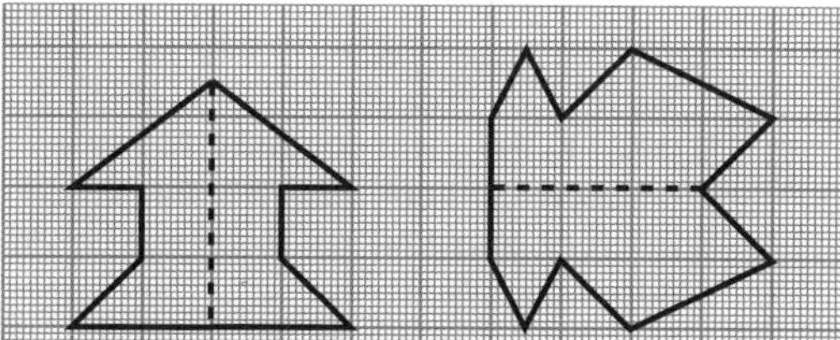

15 **48** Angles on a straight line add up to 180° so the angle for 'Beach' is 180° – 60° = 120°. There are 360° in a circle so this is $\frac{1}{3}$ of the pie chart. $144 \times \frac{1}{3} = 144 \div 3 = 48$.

16 **24** The angle for 'Sailing' is 60°, which is $\frac{1}{6}$ of the pie chart. $144 \times \frac{1}{6} = 144 \div 6 = 24$.

17 **36** The angle for 'Activity holiday' is 90°, which is $\frac{1}{4}$ of the pie chart. $144 \times \frac{1}{4} = 144 \div 4 = 36$.

18 **18** Angles on a straight line add up to 180° so the angle for 'Camping' is 180° – 90° – 45° = 45°, which is $\frac{1}{8}$ of the pie chart. $144 \times \frac{1}{8} = 144 \div 8 = 18$.

19 **18** The angle for 'Canal boat' is 45°, which is the same as for 'Camping'.

20 **£17** Add the 2 amounts of money together and divide by 2 to work out how much Ted and Zac should have if they each have the same amount (£98 + £64 = 162; 162 ÷ 2 = £81). Subtract this from Ted's amount to find how much he must give to Zac (£98 – £81 = £17).

21 **60°** Angles on a straight line add up to 180°; $2x + x = 3x$; $x = 180° \div 3 = 60°$.

22 **12°** $x = 60°$; $2x = 120°$

23 **30°** There are 90° in a right-angle; $a + a + a = 3a$; $a = 90° \div 3 = 30°$.

24 **45°** There are 90° in a right-angle; $b + b = 2b$; $b = 90° \div 2 = 45°$.

25 **£65** Round £4.98 to £5: 13 × £5 = £65

26 The function machine multiplies each number by 10 and then subtracts 1.
169 17 × 10 = 170; 170 – 1 = 169
209 21 × 10 = 210; 210 – 1 = 209
389 39 × 10 = 390; 390 – 1 = 389
449 45 × 10 = 450; 450 – 1 = 449

Mixed Paper 2

1 When rounding a number to the nearest 100, look at the number in the tens column. If it is 4 or below, leave the number in the hundreds column unchanged. If it is 5 or above, raise the number in the hundreds column by 1.
300 The 90 in 298 rounds up to 300.
800 The 40 in 847 rounds down to 800.
500 The 00 in 503 round down to 500.
1100 The 70 in 1074 rounds up to 1100

2 **49, 47, 45, 43** A quotient is the answer when you divide one number by another. First work out all the division problems (315 ÷ 7 = 45; 392 ÷ 8 = 49; 329 ÷ 7 = 47; 387 ÷ 9 = 43) and then put the quotients in order from highest to lowest.

3–4 There are 5 increments between 9.9 and 10.0. Take the difference between these numbers (10.0 – 9.9 = 0.1) and divide it by the number of increments (0.1 ÷ 5 = 0.02). Then label each increment (e.g. 9.92, 9.94, 9.96, 9.98).

3 **9.98**

4 **10.06**

5 $\mathbf{\frac{5}{6}, \frac{3}{4}, \frac{7}{12}, \frac{11}{24}, \frac{3}{8}}$
First find equivalent fractions so that the bottom numbers (the denominators) are all the same. $\frac{7}{12} = \frac{14}{24}$; $\frac{3}{8} = \frac{9}{24}$; $\frac{3}{4} = \frac{18}{24}$; $\frac{11}{24} = \frac{11}{24}$; $\frac{5}{6} = \frac{20}{24}$. Then compare the top numbers (numerators), largest first. So $\frac{20}{24} > \frac{18}{24} > \frac{14}{24} > \frac{11}{24} > \frac{9}{24}$. The fractions in order of size are $\frac{5}{6}, \frac{3}{4}, \frac{7}{12}, \frac{11}{24}, \frac{3}{8}$

6 **20 cards** For every 5 cards that Thomas has, Matthew will have 4 cards. If Matthew has 16 cards then divide this by 4 (16 ÷ 4 = 4). This shows that Matthew has his share of 4 cards multiplied by 4. Thomas' share will also be multiplied by 4 (5 × 4 = 20).

7 **18 cards** If Matthew has 16 cards and Thomas has 20 cards, there are 36 cards in total. Shared out equally, they would each receive 18 (36 ÷ 2 = 18).

8 **2650** There are 1000 metres in a kilometre: 4000 m – 1350 m = 2650 m.

9 **6** Pavel's temperature was above normal on the first Monday, the first Tuesday, Wednesday, Thursday, Friday and Saturday.

10 **1** Pavel's temperature was below normal on the second Monday.

11 **Tuesday** Pavel's temperature was highest on the first Tuesday.

12 **Thursday** Pavel's temperature began to fall on the Thursday (and did not increase again).

13 **98.4 °F** There are 10 increments between 98 and 99. Take the difference between these numbers (99 – 98 = 1) and divide it by the number of increments (1 ÷ 10 = 0.1). So each small square on the temperature axis represents 0.1 °F.

14 The coin has 2 sides (1 head and 1 tail), with an equal chance of landing on each.

15 As there are 2 sides, the chance of getting a tail is the same as the chance of getting a head.

16 **41 years 8 months** 10 + 9 + 11 + 10 = 40 years; 8 + 6 + 4 + 2 = 20 months; there are 12 months in a year, so 20 months becomes 1 year and 20 – 12 = 8 months.

17 **10 years** and **5 months** To find the mean of a set of numbers, add the numbers together and then divide the total by the quantity of numbers in the group. Deal with the years and months separately (40 ÷ 4 = 10 years; 20 ÷ 4 = 5 months).

18–22 There are 360° in a circle and 12 hours on a clock. So there are 360° ÷ 12 = 30° between each hour.

18 **6**

19 **1**

20 **4**

21 **2**

22 **5**

23 **FORWARD 4**

24 **LEFT 90°**

25 **FORWARD 3**

26 **RIGHT 90°**
FORWARD 2

27 **£4.70** To divide by a decimal fraction, it is easier to make that number a whole number. Multiply both the decimal fraction and the number you are dividing into by the same number. £7.05 ÷ 1.5 is the same as £14.10 ÷ 3 = £4.70.

28 **£16.45** £4.70 × 3.5 = £16.45

Mixed Paper 3

1 **120** 6 will divide into 12, so 6 will divide into any number that 12 will divide into. So look for a multiple of 10 that can also be divided by 8 and 12. The lowest number they all divide into is 120.

2–3 Adjust the numbers so that they have an equal amount of digits: 8 is the same as 8.000 and 2.5 is the same as 2.500.

	7		9	9	
	8	•	0	0	10
–	1	•	1	2	7
	6	•	8	7	3

		0	1	9	·	0	5
2	5	4	47	22 6	·	12	12 5

2 **6.873** 8.000 – 1.127 = 6.873

3 **19.05** 47.625 ÷ 2.5 is the same as 476.25 ÷ 25 = 19.05.

4 **9990** To multiply by 10, place the digits on a decimal grid with a 9 in the hundreds, a 9 in the tens and a 9 in the ones column. To make a digits larger, move the numbers to the left.

Mixed Papers 1–3

There is now a 9 in the thousands, a 9 in the hundreds and a 9 in the tens columns. There is nothing in the ones column, so place a zero there.

thousands	hundreds	tens	ones
9	9	9	0

5 To write these fractions as decimals, separate them from the whole number first, then write the equivalent of each fraction so that the bottom number becomes 100. Write the top number of the equivalent fraction after the decimal point. Add this back to the whole number.

4.50 $\frac{1}{2} = \frac{50}{100} = 0.50$. $4 + 0.50 = 4.50$.

7.1 $\frac{1}{10} = \frac{10}{100} = 0.10$. $7 + 0.10 = 7.10$

3.09 $\frac{9}{100} = 0.09$: $3 + 0.09 = 3.09$.

6 **4** $4 \times 4 = 16$

7 **821.5 g** There are 1000 grams in 1 kilogram; 1000 g – 178.5 g = 821.5 g

8 When plotting coordinates on a grid, use the rule "along the corridor and up the stairs" to remember to go horizontal, then vertical.

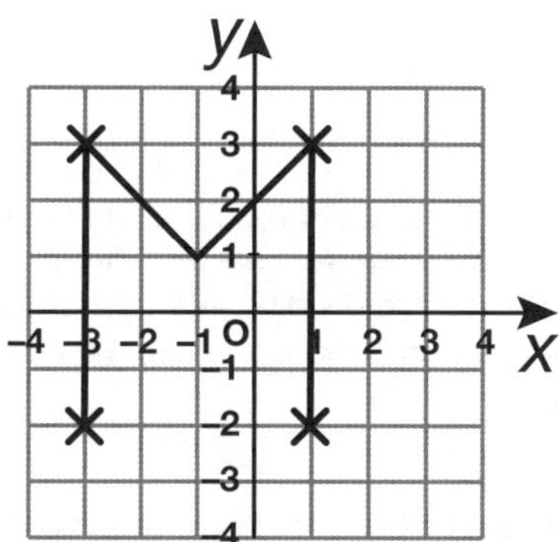

9–11 To find the mean of a set of numbers, add the numbers together and then divide the total by the quantity of numbers in the group.

9 **6** $7 + 4 + 6 + 8 + 5 = 30$; $30 \div 5 = 6$

10 **4** $3 + 2 + 7 = 12$; $12 \div 3 = 4$

11 **4** $4 + 4 + 6 + 2 = 16$; $16 \div 4 = 4$

12 $\mathbf{\frac{3}{7}}$ There are 3 white balls out of a total of $4 + 3 = 7$ balls.

13 $\mathbf{\frac{4}{7}}$ There are 4 grey balls out of a total of 7 balls.

14 **0** There are 0 black balls out of a total of 7 balls.

15 **311** The product is the result of multiplying the numbers. The sum is the result of adding the numbers. $27 \times 13 = 351$; $27 + 13 = 40$; $351 - 40 = 311$.

16 **LEFT 90°, FORWARD 1**

17 **FORWARD 1, LEFT 90°**

18 **RIGHT 90°, FORWARD 2**

19 **3, 4, 6, 12** $1 \times 12 = 12$, $2 \times 6 = 12$, $3 \times 4 = 12$

20 **2, 4, 5, 10, 20** $1 \times 20 = 20$, $2 \times 10 = 20$, $4 \times 5 = 20$

21 **1, 3, 5, 15** $1 \times 15 = 15$, $3 \times 5 = 15$

22 **2, 4**

23 **3**

24 **5**

25 **3, 4, 5** 1, 2 and 4 are factors of both 12 and 20, so the width of the box must be 1 cm, 2 cm or 4 cm. 1 and 3 are factors of both 12 and 15, so the height of the box must be 1 cm or 3 cm. 1 and 5 are factors of both 20 and 15, so the length of the box must be 1 cm or 5 cm. The right face of the cube has area of 15 cm², so the height must be 3 cm and the length 5 cm ($3 \times 5 = 15$).The top face of the box has area of 20 cm²; the length is 5 cm, so the width must be 4 cm ($5 \times 4 = 20$).

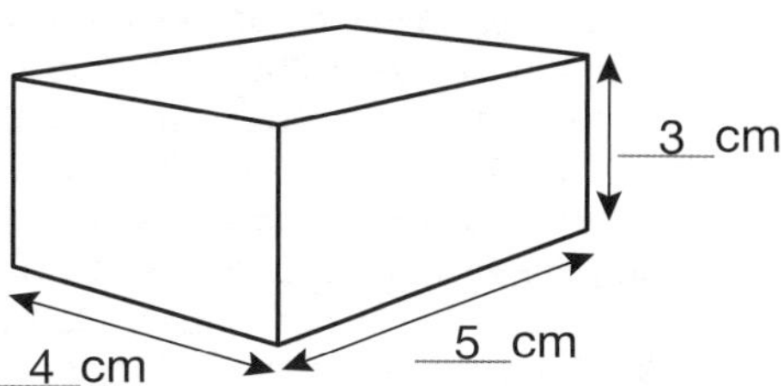

26–29 A horizontal line goes from left to right. A vertical line goes from top to bottom. Parallel lines are the same distance away from each other, all along their length. Perpendicular lines meet at a right angle.

26 **FALSE**

27 **TRUE**

28 **TRUE**

29 **TRUE**

Mixed Paper 4

1 **3, 11** of 2475, divide by 5 first. $2475 \div 5 = 495$; $495 \div 5 = 99$; $99 \div 3 = 33$; $33 \div 3 = 11$. The prime factors of 2475 are 3 and 5 and 11.

2–3 To add fractions together, first find equivalent fractions so that the bottom numbers (the denominators) are the same. Remember to only add the top numbers (the numerators), not the denominators. Deal with the whole numbers separately.

2 $\mathbf{13\frac{11}{16}}$ $7\frac{7}{8} + \frac{13}{16} = 7 + 5 + \frac{7}{8} + \frac{13}{16} = 12 + \frac{14}{16} + \frac{13}{16}$

$= 12 + \frac{27}{16} = 12 + \frac{16}{16} + \frac{11}{16}$

3 $\mathbf{3\frac{7}{15}}$ $7\frac{1}{5} - 3\frac{11}{15} = 7 - 3 + \frac{1}{5} - \frac{11}{15} = 4 + \frac{3}{15} - \frac{11}{15} =$

$4 - \frac{8}{15} = 3 + \frac{15}{15} - \frac{8}{15}$

4 **$14.60** If $1.46 is equal to £1, multiply both numbers by 10 to find out how many dollars there are for £10 ($1.46 × 10 = 14.6).

5 **11 900** If 119 shillings is equal to £1, multiply both numbers by 100 to find out how many shillings there are for £100 (119 × 100 = 11 900).

6 **€1160** If €1.16 is equal to £1, multiply both numbers by 1000 to find out how many euros there are for £1000 (1.16 × 1000 = 1160).

7 **320 cm²** To find the area of a rectangle, multiply the length by the width. The length is $8 + 4 + 8 = 20$; the width is $6 + 4 + 6 = 16$; $20 \times 16 = 320$ cm².

8 **128 cm²** Divide the cross into 3 rectangles. Find the area of each and add them together (area 1 = 4 cm × 6 cm = 24 cm²; area 2 = 20 cm × 4 cm = 80 cm²; area 3 = 4 cm × 6 cm = 24 cm²; 24 cm + 80 cm + 24 cm = 128 cm²).

9 **192 cm²** Subtract the area of the cross from the total area of the flag (320 cm² – 128 cm² = 192 cm²).

10 **72 cm** The perimeter of a rectangle can be found by adding up the 2 lengths and the 2 widths (20 + 16 + 20 + 16 = 72 cm).

11 **72 cm** The perimeter of the cross can be found by adding the length of each side (4 + 6 + 8 + 4 + 8 + 6 + 4 + 6 + 8 + 4 + 8 + 6 = 72 cm)

12 **kilometres**

13 **litres**

14 **tonnes**

15 **millimetres**

16 **B** Cube A has 1 light grey side so it cannot be a match. On the net, the dotty face and black face are in opposite positions, so cannot be adjacent, so Cube C cannot be correct either.

17 **A** Cube B has 1 side with a wavy pattern so it cannot be a match. On the net, the dotty face and black face are in opposite positions, so cannot be adjacent, so Cube C cannot be correct either.

18 **none** The net does not fold to make a cube.

19 **C** On the net, the dark grey side and the black side are in opposite positions, so cannot be adjacent, so Cube A cannot be a match. Cube B has 1 side with a wavy pattern, so cannot be correct either.

20 The pie chart is divided into 8 equal sections to cover 120 minutes. Each section represents 15 minutes (120 minutes ÷ 8 segments = 15 minutes per segment).

15 TV lasts for 1 segment × 15 minutes

30 Homework lasts for 2 segments × 15 minutes

30 Reading lasts for 2 segments × 15 minutes

15 Washing up lasts for 1 segment × 15 minutes

30 Computer time lasts for 2 segment × 15 minutes

Joanna was watching TV for 15 min, doing homework for 30 min, reading for 30 min, washing up for 15 min and was on the computer for 15 min.

21 **NOT gloss washable paint** If the answer to the question 'It is gloss?' is 'Yes' and that makes 'Gloss washable paint', then if the answer is 'No' it must make 'NOT gloss washable paint'. It is clear from the earlier question that the paint is washable, regardless of whether it is gloss or not.

22 **Is it gloss?** The 'Yes' answer to the missing question points to 'Gloss washable paint'. This answer only differs in one way from the 'No' answer: it is described as 'Gloss' while the 'No' answer is described as 'NOT gloss'. The missing question must therefore be asking whether the paint is gloss or not.

23 **30** Add up the bar heights (2 + 3 + 6 + 12 + 5 + 2 = 30)

24 **1** 2 children received 91–100 marks. 1 boy gained over 90. So 2 – 1 = 1.

25 **3** 6 children received 61–70 marks. 3 of them were girls. So $\frac{1}{2}$ of them were boys; 6 ÷ 2 = 3.

26 **1** 2 children received 41–50 marks. 1 of them were boys. So $\frac{1}{2}$ of them were girls; 2 ÷ 2 = 1.

27 **3** 12 children received 71–80 marks. 8 of them were boys. So $\frac{1}{3}$ of them were girls; 12 ÷ 4 = 3.

28 **2** 3 children received 51–60 marks. 1 of them were girls. So $\frac{2}{3}$ of them were boys; 3 ÷ 3 = 1; 2 × 1 = 2.

29 1 oz = 25 g, so multiply each of the Imperial measurements by 25 to find the Metric equivalents. The number of eggs will not change.

Ingredient	Imperial	Metric
Plain flour	5 oz	**125 g**
Semolina flour	12 oz	**300 g**
Eggs	11 eggs	**11 eggs**

30–33 The perimeter of a rectangle can be found by adding up the 2 lengths and the 2 widths.

30 **56 cm** 20 cm + 8 cm + 20 cm + 8 cm = 56 cm

31 **36 cm** 10 cm + 8 cm + 10 cm + 8 cm = 36 cm

32 **60 cm** 20 cm + 10 cm + 20 cm + 10 cm = 60 cm

33 **127 cm** 56 cm + 36 cm + 35 cm = 127 cm

Curveball Questions 2

1 **grey** Here are the steps to finding the question mark ball.
You can swap the equivalent balls, when you do, place the swapped balls underneath.

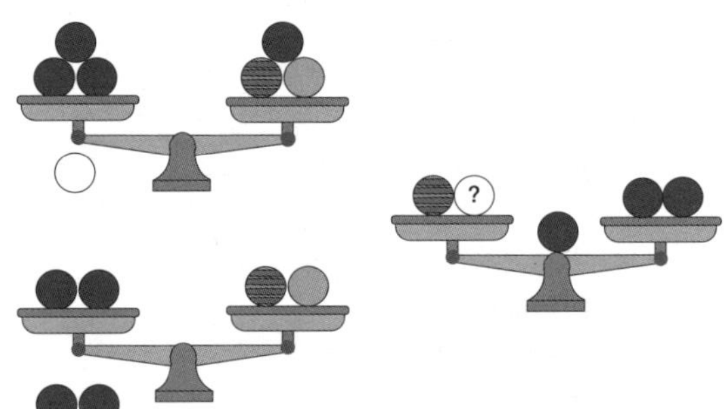

Identical balls can be added or taken from both sides. When balls are removed, place them underneath. The scales can also be doubled or tripled to get the required number of a colour on one side.

2 **10** The total of the numbers is 450, so each line is a third of that, as there are three lines, which is 150. 450 = 10 × 45, so it is 10 times the usual magic square.

The possibilities are:

50 + 90 + 10	80 + 60 + 10
90 + 20 + 40	70 + 60 + 20
50 + 80 + 20	80 + 40 + 30
50 + 70 + 30	
50 + 60 + 40	

50 appears four times, so it must be in the centre.
1, 3, 7 & 9 appear twice, so they must be in the middle of a side.
20, 40, 60 & 80 appear three times, so they must be at the corners on the diagonals.
The opposite numbers are number bonds to 100.

40	**90**	**20**
30	**50**	**70**
80	**10**	**60**

Mixed Paper 4

Curveball Questions 2

Test Paper 1

1 **0.007** 7 thousandths is 0.007
2 **2590** 200 tens 2000, 50 tens is 500 and 9 tens is 90
3 **0.14** 10 hundredths is 0.1 and 4 hundredths is 0.04
4 **33, 63**
5 $\mathbf{4^4}$
6 $\mathbf{11^5}$
7 $\mathbf{1^6}$
8 **64** There are 12 × 5 = 60 fifths in 12; 12 + 4 = 64
9 **189** To find 45% of 420, first find 10% (by dividing by 10) and then multiply the result by 4 to find 40% (420 ÷ 10 = 42; 42 × 4 = 168). Halve 10% to find 5% (42 ÷ 2 = 21). The add the result for 40% and 5% to find 45% (168 + 21 = 189).
10 **48 kg** Divide 20 kg by 5 to find $\frac{1}{12}$, then multiply by 12 to find the whole (20 kg ÷ 5 = 4 kg; 4 kg × 12 = 48 kg).
11 **6 kg** 48 kg × = 48 kg ÷ 8 = 6 kg.
12–17 To solve this type of question, make all the fractions equivalent. Here, use denominators of 100:

Mathematics	$\frac{54}{75} = \frac{16}{25} = \frac{64}{100}$
History	$\frac{27}{40} = \frac{13.5}{20} = \frac{67.5}{100}$
Geography	$\frac{39}{50} = \frac{78}{100}$
English	$\frac{48}{60} = \frac{16}{20} = \frac{80}{100}$
French	$\frac{25}{40} = \frac{12.5}{20} = \frac{62.5}{100}$
Art	$\frac{15}{20} = \frac{60}{100}$

12 **English**
13 **Geography**
14 **Art**
15 **Mathematics**
16 **History**
17 **French**
18 **45p** Divide 48p by 2 to find $\frac{1}{3}$ of the sum of money, then multiply this by 3 to find the whole (48p ÷ 2 = 24p; 24p × 3 = 72p). Then divide the whole by 8 to find $\frac{1}{8}$, then multiply by 5 to find 8 (72p ÷ 8 = 9p; 9p × 5 = 45p).
19–21 To solve a ratio, add up the ratio numbers (8 + 5 + 2 = 15). Then divide this number into the amount of money (£9.00 ÷ 15 = £0.60). Finally, multiply this number by the individual ratios.
19 **£4.80** £0.60 × 8 = £4.80
20 **£3.00** £0.60 × 5 = £3.00
21 **£1.20** £0.60 × 2 = £1.20
22–22 Find all the possible answers for the calculation on the right of the equals sign. Then work out how to make one of these possible answers on the left.
22 **–, +, –** 5 – 5 + 1 = 1 and 13 – 12 = 1
or **×, ×, +** 5 × 5 × 1 = 13 + 12
23 **+, ×, ÷** (3 + 2) × 5 = 25 and 50 ÷ 2 = 25
24–27 To find the area of a triangle, multiply the height by the length and then divide by 2.
24 **15 cm²** 6 squares long × 5 squares high = 30 cm²; 30 cm² ÷ 2 = 15 cm²
25 **14 cm²** 4 squares long × 7 squares high = 28 cm²; 28 cm² ÷ 2 = 14 cm²
26 **20 cm²** 8 squares long × 5 squares high = 40 cm²; 40 cm² ÷ 2 = 20 cm²
27 **15 cm²** 5 squares long × 6 squares high = 30 cm²; 30 cm² ÷ 2 = 15 cm²
28–30 There are 1000 metres in a kilometre, so to convert metres to kilometres, divide by 1000.
28 **1.357** 1357 m ÷ 1000 = 1.357 km
29 **12.986** 12 986 m ÷ 1000 = 12.986 km
30 **0.456** 456 m ÷ 1000 = 0.456 km
31 **9 cm²** First, find the length of each side. All four sides of a square are identical in length, so 12 cm ÷ 4 = 3 cm. Area is found by multiplying length × width, so 3 × 3 = 9 cm².
32 **64 minutes or 1 hour 4 mins** A takes 09:00 – 08:11 = 49 minutes; B takes 10:11 – 09:20 = 51 minutes; C takes 18:09 – 17:05 = 64 minutes; D takes 20:09 –19:17 = 52 minutes.
33 **A** Train A arrives in Bath at 08:45.
34 **38 minutes** 20:09 – 19:31 = 38 minutes
35 **18:09**
36 A face is a flat surface of a 3D shape, an edge is a straight line where two faces meet and a vertex is a corner where three or more faces meet.

Name of solid	Faces	Vertices	Edges
Triangular-based pyramid	4	4	6
Square-based pyramid	5	5	8
Cube	6	8	12

37–42 When reading coordinates, use the rule "along the corridor and up the stairs" to remember to go horizontal, then vertical.
37 **Long Mitton**
38 **Boston**
39 **(1, 4)**
40 **(3, 5)**
41 **20 km**
42 **40 km**
43–45

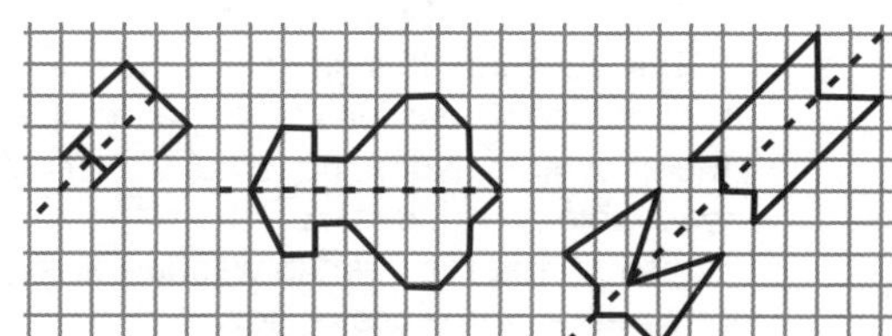

46

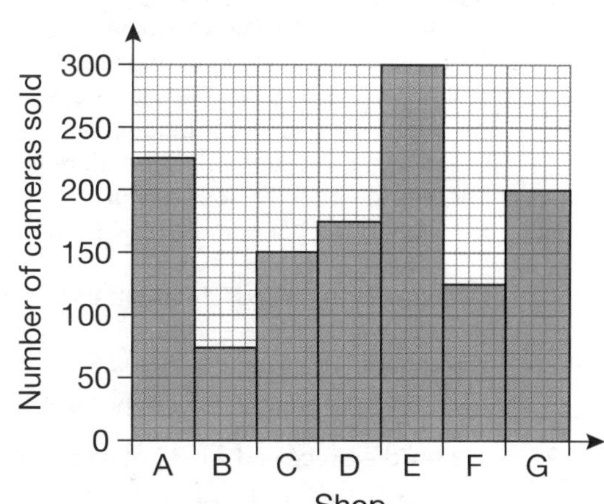

47 **4.4** The average of the 6 numbers is 4. So the total of the 6 numbers is 6 × 4 = 24. If one of the numbers is 2, the total of the remaining 5 numbers is 25 – 2 = 22. So the average of the remaining 5 numbers is 22 ÷ 5 = 4.4.

48–52 There are 360° in a circle. Here, 360° represents 72 children. 360° ÷ 72 = 5, so 5° represents 1 child.

48 **12** A right angle is 90° so the angle for 'Green' is 90° – 30° = 60°; 60 ÷ 5 = 12.

49 **33** The angle for 'Blue' is 165°; 165 ÷ 5 = 33.

50 **3** Angles on a straight line add up to 180°, so the angle for 'Orange' is 180° – 165° = 15°; 2 + 1 = 3

51 **9** A right angle is 90°, so the angle for 'Red' is half of 90°, which is 45°; 45 ÷ 5 = 9

52 **6** The angle for 'Pink' is 30°; 30 ÷ 5 = 6

53–55 To find out the probability it is helpful to write out the 6 possible scores (1, 2, 3, 4, 5, 6) and then use those numbers to answer the questions.

53 $\frac{1}{6}$ There is 1 side numbered 6 out of a total of 6.

54 $\frac{1}{6}$ There is 1 side numbered 5 out of a total of 6.

55 $\frac{1}{3}$ or $\frac{2}{6}$ There are 2 sides numbered 2 or 3 out of a total of 6.

56 **15** Add all the numbers in the oval for the Cycling Club (9 + 6 = 15).

57 **13** Add all the numbers in the oval for the Swimming Club (6 + 7 = 13).

58 **6** This is the number in the overlap of the two ovals.

59 **2** This is the number outside the ovals.

60 **16** Add the numbers that are in the two ovals, but not in the overlap (9 + 7 = 16).

61 **80** First change the metres into cm: 1 m = 100 cm, so 5 m = 500 cm and 4 m = 400 cm. Divide the length and width of the floor by the side length of a tile to find how many tiles will fit along each dimension (500 cm ÷ 50 cm = 10; 400 cm ÷ 50 cm = 8). Multiply the number of tiles that will fit along each dimension to find the number of tiles needed to tile the floor (10 × 8 = 80 tiles).

Test Paper 2

1 **10** The number of children in a class is usually about 30. This is closer to 10 than 100 or 1000.

2 **10 000** The number of people at a Premier League football match will be over 1000 but less than 100 000.

3 **3, 7** The prime factors of a number are the factors that are also prime numbers.

4 **29** 986 ÷ 34 = 29

		0	2	9
3	4	9	9 8	30 6

5 **29%** To write one number as a percentage of another, first write it as a fraction of the other. Then rewrite the fraction as an equivalent fraction with a denominator of 100 $\left(\frac{58}{200} = \frac{29}{100} = 29\%\right)$.

6–8 There are 5 increments between 0.80 and 0.81. Take the difference between these numbers (0.81 – 0.80 = 0.01) and divide it by the number of increments (0.01 ÷ 5 = 0.002). Then label each increment (e.g. 0.812, 0.814, 0.816, 0.818).

6 **0.822**

7 **0.806**

8 **0.798**

9–11 Divide a number by 1000 by moving it 3 places to the right on a place value grid.

9 **0.374** 374 ÷ 1000 = 0.374

10 **0.0148** 14.8 ÷ 1000 = 0.0148

11 **0.002** 55 2.55 ÷ 1000 = 0.002 55

12–15 Deal with the whole numbers and fractions separately. To turn a fraction into a decimal, divide the top number by the bottom number. Then add this to the whole number.

12 **3.125** 1 ÷ 8 = 0.125

13 **4.05** 1 ÷ 20 = 0.05

14 **7.625** 1 ÷ 8 = 0.625

15 **9.075** 1 ÷ 40 = 0.075

16 When a + 3 = 3, a = 0; when a = 1, a + 3 = 1 + 3 = 4; when a + 3 = 5, a = 2; when a = 3, a + 3 = 3 + 3 = 6.

a	**0**	1	**2**	3
✤	3	**4**	5	**6**

17–20 First work out the sequence between the numbers. Then use the same rule to find the next two numbers.

17 **77, 75** The sequence is to subtract 6, then subtract 5, then subtract 4 and so on; 80 – 3 = 77; 77 – 2 = 75.

18 **53, 49** The sequence is to subtract 12, the subtract 10, then subtract 8 and so on; 59 – 6 = 53; 53 – 4 = 49.

19 **45, 51** The sequence is to add 2, then add 3, then add 4 and so on; 40 + 5 = 45; 45 + 6 = 51

20 **64, 49** The sequence is decreasing square numbers (12^2, 11^2, 10^2, 9^2); 8^2 = 64; 7^2 = 49.

21 **256 cm²** To find the area of a rectangle, multiply the length by the width. In a square, the length and width are the same (16 × 16 = 256 cm²).

22 **112 cm²** Both sides of the flag are divided into 8 sections. 16 ÷ 2 = 8 so each increment represents 2 cm. Divide the cross into 3 rectangles. Find the area of each and add them together (area 1 = 4 cm × 6 cm = 24 cm²; area 2 = 16 cm × 4 cm = 64 cm²; area 3 = 4 cm × 6 cm = 24 cm²; 24 cm + 64 cm + 24 cm = 112 cm²).

23 **144 cm²** Subtract the area of the cross from the total area of the flag (256 cm² – 112 cm² = 144 cm²).

24 **64 cm** The perimeter of a rectangle can be found by adding up the 2 lengths and the 2 widths (16 + 16 + 16 + 16 = 64 cm).

25 **64 cm** The perimeter of the cross can be found by adding the length of each side (4 + 6 + 6 + 4 + 6 + 6 + 4 + 6 + 6 + 4 + 6 + 6 = 64 cm).

26 **miles**
27 **pints** or **fluid ounces**
28 **ounces**
29 **inches** or **feet and inches**
30 The perimeter of a rectangle can be found by adding up the 2 lengths and the 2 widths. For a square, the length and width are the same.

	Length	Width	Perimeter
Rectangle 1	18 cm	**2 cm**	40 cm
Rectangle 2	**12 cm**	3 cm	30 cm
Rectangle 3	9 cm	4 cm	**26 cm**
Square	6 cm	**6 cm**	**24 cm**

31–35 All the places shown are ahead of London. To find the time in one of the other places, add the correct number of hours to the time in London. To find the time in London, subtract the correct number of hours from the time in one of the other places.
31 **10:00 p.m.** 10:00 a.m. + 12 hours = 10:00 p.m.
32 **2:30 p.m.** London + 5 hours = 2:30 p.m.
33 **1:30 p.m.** 3:30 p.m. – 2 hours = 1:30 p.m.
34 **12:15 p.m.** 1:15 p.m. – 1 hour = 12:15 p.m.
35 **5:30 p.m.** It is 2 hours later in India than in Kenya. 3:00 p.m. + 2 = 5:30 p.m.
36

You start facing	turn through	clockwise /anticlockwise	you are now facing
W	135°	anticlockwise	**SE**
SE	45°	clockwise	**S**
NE	90°	anticlockwise	**NW**
SW	45°	anticlockwise	**S**
S	180°	clockwise	**N**

37 **cube**
38 **triangular-based pyramid**
39 **cuboid**
40 **triangular prism**
41–44 If a shape has a line of symmetry, the sides on either side of the line will be identical.
41 **H**
42 **B, D, E, G**
43 **A**
44 **C**
45 **10**
46 **5 km**
47 **5 km**
48 **12 km/h** 2 km in 10 minutes; 6 × 10 minutes = 60 minutes; 2 × 6 = 12 km in 1 hour.
49 **14** The mode is the most popular number. Two people have 14 CDs.
50 **13** To find the median of a set of numbers, put the numbers in order from smallest to largest (5, 8, 12, 14, 14, 19). The median is the middle number. If there are 2 middle numbers, add the 2 numbers together and then divide by 2 (12 + 14 = 26; 26 ÷ 2 = 13).
51 **14** To find the range, subtract the smallest number from the largest number (19 – 5 = 14).
52 **12** To find the mean of a set of numbers, add the numbers together and then divide the total by the quantity of numbers in the group (8 + 5 + 14 + 19 + 14 + 12 = 72; 72 ÷ 6 = 12).
53 **75%** $\frac{1}{2}$ of the pupils have one computer and $\frac{1}{4}$ have more than one computer; $\frac{1}{2} + \frac{1}{4} = \frac{3}{4}$
54 $\mathbf{\frac{1}{4}}$
55 **8** $\frac{1}{4}$ of the pupils have no computer; $32 \times \frac{1}{4} =$ 32 ÷ 4 = 8.
56 **24** of the pupils have at least one computer; $32 \times \frac{3}{4} = 32 \div 4 \times 3 = 24$.
57–58 To find probability it is helpful to write out the 6 possible scores (1, 2, 3, 4, 5, 6) and then use those numbers to answer the questions.
57 $\mathbf{\frac{1}{3}}$ There are two sides numbered 4 or 5 out of a 6, and $\frac{2}{6} = \frac{1}{3}$.
58 **1** There are 6 sides numbered 1, 2, 3, 4, 5 and 6, so this is certain and $\frac{6}{6} = 1$.
59 **49 cm²** The four sides of a square are the same length, so divide 28 cm by 4 to find the length of 1 side (28 cm ÷ 4 = 7 cm). Multiply the side length by itself to find the area (7 cm × 7 cm = 49 cm²).
60 **350, 280** To solve a ratio, add up the ratio numbers (5 + 4 = 9). The divide this number into the number of children (630 ÷ 9 = 70). Finally, multiply this number by the individual ratios (5 × 70 = 350 boys; 4 × 70 = 280 girls).